GW00703534

Intext **Series in**
PSYCHOLOGICAL ASSESSMENT

HAROLD J. VETTER—CONSULTING EDITOR

Florida State University

Statistics for Educational Measurement

Statistics for Educational Measurement

THOMAS R. KNAPP

Professor of Education
University of Rochester

INTEXT EDUCATIONAL PUBLISHERS

COLLEGE DIVISION

Scranton Toronto London

Isbn 0-7002-2373-8

Library of Congress Catalog Card Number 73-151646

Copyright ©,1971, by International Textbook Company

TO

PHILLIP J. RULON

Preface

Most textbooks in educational measurement treat classroom test construction, standardized tests, measurement principles, and statistical analysis all within the same volume. The present text is restricted to a discussion of statistical concepts related to basic measurement problems.

This book is intended primarily for undergraduate and graduate students in education who take a course in educational or psychological measurement without having taken a prior course in statistics. Such students often find the statistical aspects of measurement particularly difficult to comprehend.

The text is written in the first person (singular and plural), because I feel strongly that textbooks conceived as teaching devices should be written that way. The impersonal third person is fine for textbooks designed to serve primarily as reference sources.

I have dedicated this book to the late Phillip J. Rulon of the Harvard Graduate School of Education, my former adviser and friend. Whatever merits the book may possess are primarily the fruits of his influence on my professional development. The mistakes are all my fault, not his.

Thomas R. Knapp

Rochester, N.Y.
March, 1971

Preface

Contents

Statistics for Educational Measurement

The Measurement
Problem

I like to think about the measurement of human beings in the following way:

Suppose that we could hang a large number of tags around the neck of each person in the world. On each tag there would be the name of an attribute– height, musical aptitude, beauty, religious affiliation– and a number, which for quantitative attributes would indicate how much of the attribute the person possessed and for qualitative attributes would indicate into which category he fell.

We would be able to survey at any time how many people possessed how much of each attribute or fell into each category. The process of selection of individuals for certain tasks would be a routine mechanical matter of reading tags and shuffling people. Those individuals who had high numbers on particular tags would be assigned to a task where those attributes were important; those individuals who had appropriate patterns of numbers on another set of tags would be assigned to some other task where such patterns were relevant.

The major problem encountered in this approach to Utopia is the determination of which numbers to put on which tags. Why is this such a problem? Here are just a few of the reasons:

1. The actual measurement procedure used to "get at" the attribute may not be the proper procedure to use. Individuals who in fact possess a large amount of a given trait may not receive large numbers when the procedure is used on them and those who have a small amount of the trait may not receive small numbers. This is the problem of *validity*.

2. Most traits are subject to changes with time, and

changes dependent upon the specific "items" that comprise the measuring instrument, so that a score assigned to an individual based on a given instrument at a given point in time may not be the "true" score that the individual really "deserves."   This is the problem of *reliability*.

3. Inherent in most measurement processes is the necessity for one person to make judgments as to the scores that should be assigned to a group of individuals to whom the measuring instrument has been applied. The scores assigned by this person may differ from the scores assigned by a second person. Moreover, the first person in reevaluating the same group of individuals may not agree with his own initial scores. This is the problem of *objectivity*.[1]

4. In the selection of a measuring instrument, one must be concerned with the cost of such a device in terms of time, money, or effort, and with the availability of a proper basis for interpretation of the measurements obtained. This is the problem of *practicability*.

To illustrate:

Johnny, age 13, takes a scientific aptitude test at the beginning of ninth grade and gets a score of 64, so he would have a tag which reads "Scientific Aptitude, 64." But . . .

1. How do we know that this test actually measures scientific aptitude? It may look as though it does—the title says so, the authors are reputable in their field, the items are relevant—but do people who score well on this test do well in science, and do people who do not score well on this test fail to do well in science?

2. If Johnny were to take this test (or an equivalent form thereof) a second time, would his performance on the second occasion be quite similar to his performance on the first occasion, or would the two performances be quite different?

---

[1] Many authors use the term "scorer reliability" or "reader reliability" rather than "objectivity." I prefer to restrict the use of the word "reliability" to situations involving random errors relevant to the individual and the test, not to the *scoring* of the test.

3. If another person were to score Johnny's test, would he also give him a score of 64? If the same person who scored Johnny's test were to rescore it, would he arrive at a score of 64 again?
4. 64 what? Right answers? Out of a possible how many? How does his score compare with the scores obtained by other 13-year olds? By other ninth-graders?

Suppose that in seeking information concerning the foregoing queries, we discover that:

Johnny answered 64 questions correctly out of 75 questions on the test, all of which were of the completion ("fill-in-the-blanks") variety. He scored at the 76th percentile compared to a sample of one hundred and thirty-seven 13-year-olds (i.e., his score was higher than the scores obtained by 76 percent of the students in that sample), and at the 89th percentile compared to a sample of 118 ninth-graders. All papers were scored twice by each of two independent scorers. Scorer X gave Johnny 61 and 69; scorer Y gave him 54 and 72 (the average of all of these numbers is 64). Johnny was given an equivalent form of the test the following day and got a score of 73 (again an average of four scorings). The test has been attacked by the critics. Correlations between scores on this test and grades in secondary school science courses range from - .17 to .21.

Suppose, on the other hand, that we discover the following:

Johnny answered 91 questions correctly out of 125 questions on the test, all of which were of the true-false variety. He answered 27 questions incorrectly and omitted 7 questions, his score of 64 being arrived at by subtracting the number of wrong answers, 27, from the number of right answers, 91, according to the standard "correction-for-guessing" formula. He scored at the 43rd percentile compared to a representative national sample of 10,000 13-year-olds, and at the 41st percentile compared to a like sample of 12,000 ninth-graders. All papers were machine-scored twice, and 64 was the score obtained on both occasions. Johnny was given an alternate form of the test the following day and got a score of 66 (93 right, 27 wrong, 5 omits). The test has been warmly received by the critics. Correlations with science grades range from .49 to .67.

It would seem that in the first instance Johnny did quite well on a poor test. In the second instance Johnny was slightly below average on a good test. Yet the raw datum—a score of 64 on a scientific aptitude test—is the same in both cases.

These four "subproblems" constitute a convenient taxonomy for the study of educational measurement. They also serve as the four criteria which a good measuring instrument must meet: it must be valid, reliable, objective, and practicable.

In the evaluation of an educational test with respect to these criteria many different statistical techniques are utilized. The remaining chapters of this book are devoted to a treatment of some of the concepts which are useful in making such evaluations.

chapter 2

Probability

"The probability of getting a 2 in one roll of a single die is 1/6." "The probability of dying before age 42 if alive at age 41 is .01." "The probability of pulling through this operation is .80."

The word "probability" is used in many different contexts by many different people. There are at least three ways of "thinking about" probability, and the above quotations illustrate the various approaches to this concept.

A. DEFINITION

One definition of the word "probability" is the *a priori*, or *deductive*, definition. By this definition, the probability of any particular result, say A, is equal to the number of ways A can take place divided by the total number of equally likely results. In symbols,

$$P(A) = \frac{m}{n} \tag{2-1}$$

where m is the number of ways A can take place and n is the total number of equally likely results.

The first quotation above is an application of this definition of probability. Let A be the result "getting a 2 in one roll of a single die." The number of ways m you can get a 2 in one roll of a single die, is 1, for only one of the faces of the die has two dots. The total number of equally likely results for one roll of a single die n is 6, since the die has six faces and by intuitive appeal to the symmetrical construction of the die, each of the faces is as likely to appear as the top face as any other. Therefore the probability of getting a 2—that is, $P(A)$, is equal to m/n or 1/6.

This example brings out the deductive nature of this approach to probability. On the basis of the symmetry of the situation one argues that the probability is 1/6, the interpretation being that one out of every six rolls of the die should result in a 2 on the top face. The crucial thing is that the probability statement is made *without ever actually rolling the die.* One may be encouraged to roll the die several times in order to confirm the statement, but this is not essential to the specification of the probability of the result.

The *a priori* definition of probability applies only to results which are concerned with symmetrical "objects" such as dice, coins, or cards, since the phrase "equally likely results" doesn't make any sense in an asymmetrical situation. For example, if one were interested in the probability that a thumbtack would land on its head (with point up), this definition would not apply, as there is no valid basis for the argument that the two possible results, viz., point up and point down (on its side), are equally likely.

Some people reject this definition of probability on the grounds that it is circular—that it defines probability in terms of the concept of "equally likelihood" which is itself "probabilistic." Others claim it is not circular, because the total number of "equally likely" results is determined deductively by an appeal to the symmetry of the die, coin, or deck of cards, under consideration.

A second definition of probability is the *empirical*, or *relative frequency*, definition. According to this definition, the probability of any result A is the limiting value of the ratio of the number of times A took place to the total number of results obtained, for a very large total number of results. In symbols,

$$P(A) = \lim_{n \to \infty} \frac{m}{n} \qquad (2\text{-}2)$$

where m is the number of times A took place, n is the total number of results obtained, and the symbol $\to \infty$ means "gets very large."

Now this definition looks and sounds very much like the *a priori* definition, but there are three very important differences between the two. First, the tenses of the verbs used in the definitions are different. The *a priori* definition talks about "*can take* place" whereas the relative frequency definition talks about "*took* place." The distinction here is that this second definition requires that data concerning the occurrence and nonoccurrence of A must be available *before* one can talk about its probability. This was not the case for the first definition.

Secondly, the expressions "limiting value" and "a very large total number of results" appear in the relative frequency definition. This is to assure that the statement concerning the probability of A is based on an adequate amount of information rather than a few scattered trials.

Finally, this definition avoids the question of "equally likely" results, thereby removing the possible circularity of the *a priori* definition and permitting the concept to be extended to asymmetric situations.

The second quotation at the beginning of this chapter is an example of "this kind" of probability. Certainly there is no *a priori* reasoning one can use to determine the probability of death. All statements concerning such probabilities must be made on the basis of mortality tables for a large, representative segment of the population of concern.

The thumbtack problem referred to above is also an example of a situation requiring the relative frequency approach to probability. If one is interested in the probability that a thumbtack will land point up, one has no choice but to throw the thumbtack a large number of times, recording both the number of times the thumbtack landed point up and the total number of tosses, dividing the former by the latter. *From then on* this figure is used as the probability that in the future that particular thumbtack will land point up.

Note that this second definition of probability also "works" for symmetrical objects and situations. For example, if one just happens to have an "ideal" coin for which the *a priori* probability of "heads" is 1/2, and one were to toss this coin a thousand times, the ratio of the number of heads to the total number of tosses would be very close to 1/2. Similarly, if one were to roll a perfectly balanced die a large number of times, one would find that the proportion of 2's would be very close to 1/6.

But the real beauty of this definition is that it also works for "loaded" coins and dice, and stacked decks of cards! For example, if one has a given coin of particular interest with unknown balance, one could determine the probability that *this particular coin* would land heads. Depending upon the actual amount of imbalance the numerical result might be very close to 1/2 or quite deviant from it.

The third definition of probability is the *subjective*, or *personal*, definition. According to this definition, an individual ascribes to any result *A* a number from 0 to 1 which is a measure of that individual's strength of conviction that *A* will take place. This number may or may not correspond to the *a priori* measure, if one can be determined, and may or may not correspond to the relative frequency measure, if *it* can be determined. Finally, the number ascribed may differ from individual to individual.

The final quotation at the beginning of this chapter is an example of personal probability. This statement, which is similar to the kind of statement often made by or at least attributed to doctors in communicating with the relatives and friends of surgical patients, represents one man's opinion concerning the success of a serious operation. Certainly there is no *a priori* basis for such a statement; and since the patient will not be subjected to this particular operation a large number of times (as a matter of fact, it may be the only such operation ever performed), the relative frequency definition of probability also breaks down. If one insists on saying something about the likelihood of survival it must be a subjective statement.

Many people reject this definition of probability as unnecessary and meaningless, and in recent years there has developed a great controversy between the advocates of personal probability, who usually call themselves "Bayesian" statisticians (derived from the name of Thomas Bayes, whose mathematical theorem is part of the controversy), and those who restrict the concept of probability to things which are amenable to repeated trials, who are known as "classical" statisticians.

As far as educational measurement is concerned, the first two definitions of probability are sufficient. In the discussion below concerning the problem of chance success on a test the *a priori* definition will be assumed throughout.

Regardless of the definition adopted, the probability of any result A is a number between 0 and 1, where 0 denotes impossibility, 1 denotes certainty. Results having probabilities less than 1/2, or .5, are less likely to happen than not; those having probabilities greater than 1/2 are more likely to happen than not.

B. THE PROBABILITY OF 'NOT A' AND THE CONCEPT OF "ODDS"

Since a probability of 1 represents certainty, and since, in line with the usual principles of logic, a result A must either take place or not take place, we know that

$$P(A) + P(\text{not } A) = 1 \qquad (2\text{-}3)$$

where "not A" is the result "A will not take place." For example, the probability of rolling a 2 in one roll of a die is 1/6. The probability of not rolling a 2—that is, rolling a 1, 3, 4, 5, or 6 is 5/6, since it is certain that one of these numbers must come up.

The relation $P(A) + P(\text{not } A) = 1$ is very useful in the solution of probability problems. If we know $P(A)$, we can find $P(\text{not } A)$ by transposing $P(A)$ to the right side of the equation, obtaining $P(\text{not } A) = 1 - P(A)$. Similarly, if we know $P(\text{not } A)$, and this happens more often than you might expect, we can find $P(A)$ by a similar transposition, viz., $P(A) = 1 - P(\text{not } A)$.

Many people confuse the concepts of "probability of" and "odds against." If $P(A)$ is the probability of some result A, then *the odds against A* are determined as

$$\text{odds vs. } A = \frac{P(\text{not } A)}{P(A)} = \frac{1 - P(A)}{P(A)} \qquad (2\text{-}4)$$

For example, let A be the result "drawing a spade in one draw of one card from a deck of cards." Since there are 13 spades in the deck, and 52 cards altogether, $P(A) = 13/52 = 1/4$. From the above, odds vs. $A = \dfrac{1 - P(A)}{P(A)} = \dfrac{3/4}{1/4} = 3/1$, or "3 to 1"; i.e., the odds against drawing a spade are 3 to 1. Knowing that the odds against a particular result are 3 to 1, a common error is to report the probability of the result as 1/3 rather than 1/4.

C. "AND" AND "OR" PROBABILITIES

The definitions of probability treated above apply to what are known as "simple" probabilities (here "simple" does not necessarily mean "easy"!), since each of the definitions applies to the probability of a particular result in *one* toss of *one* coin, *one* roll of *one* die, *one* draw of *one* card, etc. Quite often we are concerned with more complex phenomena such as the probability of fewer than two heads in four tosses of a coin, the probability of getting a 7 in one roll of two dice, or the probability of at least 3 spades out of 13 cards. When the result with which we are concerned involves more than one occurrence and/or more than one trial, the calculation of the probability of the result can become quite involved. Fortunately there are a number of rules to aid in the calculations.

1. The "And" Rules

If we want to determine the probability of a result of the form "*A* and *B*" and we know the simple probabilities of *A* and *B*, respectively, we can determine $P(A \text{ and } B)$ as follows:

$P(A \text{ and } B) = P(A)$ times $P(B$, given that A has taken place)

which is usually written

$$P(A \text{ and } B) = P(A) \cdot P(B/A) \tag{2-5}$$

For example, consider the following problem: If 2 cards are drawn from a deck of cards, what is the probability that they will both be spades?

In order to solve this problem, let A be the result "the first card is a spade" and let B be the result "the second card is a spade." By the rule just given:

The probability that both cards are spades = P(first card is a spade *and* second card is a spade) = $P(A \text{ and } B) = P(A)$ times $P(B$, given that A has taken place) = $13/52 \cdot 12/51 = 1/17$, since in considering the draw of the first card there are 13 spades and 52 cards, while for the second card there are only 12 spades (given that the first card drawn is a spade) and only 51 cards.

In the solution to this problem the stated conditions were such that we made the implicit assumption that the first card drawn was not replaced in the deck before the second card was drawn. If the first card *were* replaced, the answer to the problem would be different. We would have, defining A and B as before:

$P(A$ and $B) = 13/52 \cdot 13/52 = 1/16$, since for each draw the probability of a spade is the same, there being 13 spades and 52 cards on each occasion.

In the latter case, the probability of "B, given that A has taken place" is determined in exactly the same way we would determine it even if A did *not* take place, and is equal to $P(B)$ itself. Thus the occurrence of B is *independent* of the occurrence of A in this instance. Whenever two results A and B are independent, the "and" rule simplifies to the following form:

$$P(A \text{ and } B) = P(A) \cdot P(B) \qquad (2\text{-}6)$$

Both the nonindependent and the independent cases of the "and" rule can be extended to problems involving three or more simple results, as follows:

In general,

$$P(A \text{ and } B \text{ and } C \text{ and} \ldots) = P(A) \cdot P(B/A) \cdot P(C/A \text{ and } B) \cdots$$
$$(2\text{-}7)$$

If $A, B, C, \ldots$ are all independent,

$$P(A \text{ and } B \text{ and } C \text{ and} \ldots) = P(A) \cdot P(B) \cdot P(C) \cdots \quad (2\text{-}8)$$

2. The "Or" Rules

If we want to determine the probability of a result of the form "A or B" and we know the simple probabilities of A and B, respectively, we can determine $P(A$ or $B)$ as

$$P(A \text{ or } B) = P(A) + P(B) - P(A \text{ and } B) \qquad (2\text{-}9)$$

For example, consider the following problem: If 1 card is drawn from a deck of cards, what is the probability that it is either an ace or a spade?

Let A be "card is an ace" and B "card is a spade." By the "or" rule:

The probability that the card drawn is either an ace or a spade $= P(A$ or $B) = P(A) + P(B) - P(A$ and $B) = 4/52 + 13/52 - 1/52 = 16/52 = 4/13$, since

(a) there are 4 aces and 52 cards

(b) there are 13 spades and 52 cards

(c) there is only 1 card out of the 52 cards that is both an ace and a spade, and that is, of course, the ace of spades[1]

The reason for "subtracting off" the quantity 1/52 is that the ace of spades has been counted twice in the first two terms on the right-hand side of the equation, once as an ace and once as a spade.

Consider this problem: If one card is drawn from a deck of cards, what is the probability that it is either an ace or a king?

Letting A be "card is an ace" and B "card is a king," we have:

$P(A \text{ or } B) = P(A) + P(B) - P(A \text{ and } B) = 4/52 + 4/52 - 0 = 8/52 = 2/13$, since:

(a) there are 4 aces and 52 cards
(b) there are 4 kings and 52 cards
(c) *there is no card* which is both an ace and a king; we are only drawing 1 card—it may be an ace, it may be a king, it may be one of the 11 other denominations, but it can't be two different denominations at the same time

Whenever $P(A \text{ and } B) = 0$, the results A and B are said to be *mutually exclusive*—that is, they can't both occur at the same time. In this event, the "or" rule reduces to the following:

$$P(A \text{ or } B) = P(A) + P(B) \qquad (2\text{-}10)$$

Both the nonmutually exclusive and the mutually exclusive cases of the "or" rule can be extended to the situation involving three or more simple results. For example, for three results A, B, and C:

In general,

$$\begin{aligned} P(A \text{ or } B \text{ or } C) = P(A) + P(B) + P(C) &- P(A \text{ and } B) \\ &- P(A \text{ and } C) - P(B \text{ and } C) \\ &+ P(A \text{ and } B \text{ and } C) \end{aligned} \qquad (2\text{-}11)$$

If A, B, and C are mutually exclusive,

$$P(A \text{ or } B \text{ or } C) = P(A) + P(B) + P(C) \qquad (2\text{-}12)$$

---

[1] For this example $P(A \text{ and } B)$ can also be determined by the "and" rule above, as follows: $P(\text{ace and spade}) = P(\text{ace}) \cdot P(\text{spade, given ace}) = 4/52 \cdot 1/4 = 1/52$.

D. THE PROBLEM OF CHANCE SUCCESS ON A TEST

The foregoing discussion of probability has been couched in terms of coins, dice, and cards. This is all well and good, since the theory of probability originally arose out of problems involving games of chance, and since it is relatively easy to introduce the basic ideas of probability in these contexts. But so far as this particular book is concerned, of much greater importance is the application of probabilistic reasoning to situations involving educational tests. We shall now turn to such an application.

Educational tests, both "teacher-made" and "standardized," are often of the "objective" variety—true-false, multiple-choice, or matching—wherein the student selects his answer to each question from among a number of answers provided by the test author (as opposed to the completion or essay types of examinations wherein the student must compose his own answers). Since on this sort of test all of the answers appear in the questions themselves and the student's task is to pick out the ones he thinks correctly answer the questions, there is always the possibility that a student can get one or more correct answers merely by guesswork. For example, if a test contains 100 true-false (two-choice) questions with "true" being the correct answer to 50 of the questions and "false" being the correct answer to the other 50 questions, a student who checks "true" for all of the 100 questions, without even reading the questions, will obtain 50 correct answers and 50 incorrect answers—that is, he will get half of the questions right even if he has absolutely no knowledge whatsoever about the material being tested.

This phenomenon is not so pronounced when the number of choices for each question is rather large, say five or more, but even with five choices a student who guesses at the answer to each question will get about 1/5 or 20 percent of the questions right. (I say "about," rather than "exactly," since it all depends on whether or not each of the choices appears as the correct answer an equal number of times, and on the particular guessing "strategy" employed by the student.)

In evaluating educational tests and interpreting scores obtained on educational tests, one must constantly be aware of this matter of "chance" success. Many measurement specialists argue that if a test consists of choice-type items, the scores obtained on such a test should be *corrected* by a special formula which takes into account this possibility of chance success. There has been a great deal of controversy concerning whether or not this "correction-for-guessing" formula is justified, necessary, or desirable, and when it should be used and when it should not be used. I prefer not to get embroiled in that controversy in this book, and refer the interested reader to other measurement texts (e.g., Ebel, 1965). But since the derivation of this formula involves an application of the concept of probability to educational tests, I shall go through it step-by-step.

First we need some notation:

Let R be the number of questions on a test that a student answers correctly (the "rights").

Let W be the number of questions on a test that a student answers incorrectly (the "wrongs").

Let A be the number of questions on a test that a student answers altogether $(= R + W)$.[2]

Let C be the number of choices for each question.

We want to develop a formula for estimating K, the number of questions for which the student actually "knows" the correct answer.

A student will answer correctly those questions for which he knows the correct answer *plus* those questions for which he successfully guesses the correct answer. The number of "don't knows," i.e., the number of questions he chooses to guess at, is equal to $A - K$. If each of these questions has C choices, we would expect, by *a priori* probabilistic reasoning, that the student would get 1/Cth of these right, or $\dfrac{A - K}{C}$. Therefore, we have

$$K + \frac{A - K}{C} = R$$

Our problem is to solve this equation for K. By straightforward algebra,

Multiplying through by C $CK + (A - K) = CR$
Removing the parenthesis and
  substituting $R + W$ for A $CK + R + W - K = CR$

---

[2] In the derivation of this formula we need not be concerned with the number of questions he omits.

Factoring a K out of CK and K	$K(C - 1) + R + W = CR$
Transposing R and W to the opposite side of the equation	$K(C - 1) = CR - R - W$
Factoring an R out of CR and R	$K(C - 1) = R(C - 1) - W$
Dividing through by $C - 1$	$K = R - \dfrac{W}{C - 1}$ (2-13)

This is the traditional "correction-for-guessing" formula. To estimate the number of items for which a student actually knows the correct answer, one subtracts from the total number of right answers the number of wrong answers divided by one less than the number of choices. For example, if a student gets 50 right answers and 50 wrong answers on a true-false test ($C = 2$), his corrected score is $50 - \dfrac{50}{2 - 1} = 50 - 50 = 0$. This is intuitively satisfying, as a student who checks "true" for all questions on a 100-item test would get 50 of them right just by chance; such a performance merits a score of 0.

As a less extreme example, consider the following: A student gets 29 right and 12 wrong on a 5-choice test. His corrected score is

$$29 - \frac{12}{5 - 1} = 29 - \frac{12}{4} = 29 - 3 = 26$$

E. DECISION MAKING AND TYPE I AND TYPE II ERRORS

In education, as well as in all behavioral sciences, it is necessary to make a great many decisions in instances wherein we are not perfectly sure of the correctness of our actions. For example, we decide to use the "look-say" method of reading rather than the phonetic method, even though the evidence in favor of the former method is not overwhelming. Or we decide against closed-circuit television in all of our classrooms, even though this technique has been found to be useful in some situations. We shall always have to make decisions under uncertainty. Sometimes we will make the "right" decisions; sometimes we will make the "wrong" decisions. We shall never be able to eliminate errors (wrong decisions), but with a knowledge of probabilities we can improve our "batting average" and we can determine *how often* we are likely to be wrong.

The following example is designed to illustrate this matter of decision and error:

You have constructed a 20-item quiz, each item consisting of a four-choice multiple-choice question. Before you administer the test you announce to your class that the purpose of this test is diagnostic—you want to find out who is progressing satisfactorily and who is not, as far as knowledge of the content of a certain unit of instruction is concerned. You define "progressing satisfactorily" as a grasp of 70 percent or more of the material; you define "not progressing satisfactorily" as a grasp of the material equivalent to sheer guesswork. Your task is to set the cutting point that will separate the "guessers" from the "knowers." The problem is: what score on this quiz is such that, if a student scores less than this amount you can say with reasonable assurance that he is just guessing, whereas if he scores more than this amount you can say with equal assurance that he has at least a 70 percent command of the material?

The answer to this problem can be determined by applying some of the concepts treated earlier in this chapter. If we let A be the result "getting the right answer to any of the 20 items," the problem becomes one of deciding for what range of scores it is likely that $P(A) = 1/4$, or .25 (the guessers), and for what range of scores it is likely that $P(A) = 7/10$, or .70 (the knowers). Common sense tells us that the cutting point should fall somewhere between 1/4 of 20, which is 5, and 7/10 of 20, which is 14. But where should it be?

Let us define "passing" the test as the obtaining of a score which equals or exceeds the to-be-determined cutting point and "failing" the test as the obtaining of a score which falls below the cutting point.

1. Is a Score of 6 an Appropriate Cutting Point?

Consider the guesser. The probability that a guesser will get a score of 6 or more = the probability of 6 or 7 or 8 or . . . 20 correct answers by chance = $P(6) + P(7) + P(8) + \cdots + P(20)$, for $P(A) = 1/4$, since the results 6 right, 7 right, 8 right, etc. are mutually exclusive. Now there are many ways a student can get 6 right answers. He could get the first 6 right and the last 14 wrong; the first 14 wrong and the last 6 right; the first 2 right, the next 10 wrong, the next 4 right, and the last 4 wrong; etc.

It turns out that the number of ways of getting 6 rights and 14 wrongs out of 20 items is the number of *permutations* of 20 things, 6 of which are of one kind and 14 of which are of a second kind, which is equal to 38760.

The probability of each of these sequences of right and wrong answers—for example, the pattern RRRRRRWWWWWW-WWWWWWWW, is, by the generalization of the "and" rule for independent results (it is not unreasonable to assume that the items are independent):

$$1/4 \cdot 1/4 \cdot 1/4 \cdot 1/4 \cdot 1/4 \cdot 1/4 \cdot 3/4 \cdot 3/4 \cdot 3/4 \cdot 3/4 \cdot 3/4$$
$$\cdot 3/4 \cdot 3/4 \cdot 3/4 \cdot 3/4 \cdot 3/4 \cdot 3/4 \cdot 3/4 \cdot 3/4 \cdot 3/4$$
$$= (1/4)^6 (3/4)^{14} = .000004349$$

Since each of the possible sequences of 6 rights and 14 wrongs is mutually exclusive of the other sequences,

$$P(6) = .000004349 + .000004349 + .000004349$$
$$+ \cdots (38760 \text{ times})$$
$$= 38760 (.000004349) = .1686$$

Similarly,[3]

$P(7) = .1124$	$P(11) = .0030$
$P(8) = .0609$	$P(12) = .0008$
$P(9) = .0271$	$P(13) = .0002$
$P(10) = .0099$	$P(14) = P(15) = \cdots = P(20) = 0$
	(to 4 decimal places)

Therefore,

$$P(6 \text{ or more}) = .1686 + .1124 + .0609 + .0271 + .0099$$
$$+ .0030 + .0008 + .0002$$
$$= .3829$$

This is the probability that a guesser would "pass" the test. The probability that a guesser would "fail" the test is equal to $1 - .3829 = .6171$.

---

[3] These probabilities have been taken from *Tables of the Binomial Probability Distribution* (1949). The calculations involved in this example are obviously very difficult. Fortunately these calculations and other similar calculations have been carried out once and for all and the results have been compiled in readily available tables.

Now consider the knower. The reasoning is exactly the same as for the guesser except that the probability of a "right" answer for any item is 7/10 rather than 1/4 and the probability of a "wrong" answer is 3/10 rather than 3/4. Thus, for the knower,

$$P(6) = 38760(7/10)^6 \ (3/10)^{14}$$

$$= .0002$$

Also,

$P(7) = .0010$	$P(12) = .1144$	$P(17) = .0716$
$P(8) = .0039$	$P(13) = .1643$	$P(18) = .0278$
$P(9) = .0120$	$P(14) = .1916$	$P(19) = .0068$
$P(10) = .0308$	$P(15) = .1789$	$P(20) = .0008$
$P(11) = .0654$	$P(16) = .1304$	

Therefore,

$$P(6 \text{ or more}) = .0002 + .0010 + .0039 + \cdots + .0008$$

$$= .9999$$

This is the probability that a knower would pass the test. The probability that a knower would fail the test is equal to 1 - .9999 = .0001.

To return to the question—is a score of 6 an appropriate cutting point? If the purpose of the test is to separate the guessers from the knowers, one criterion of "appropriate" is that the probability of a guesser's passing the test is equal to the probability of a knower's failing the test, for we would like to be able to identify the two with equal assurance. From the foregoing calculations,

$$P(\text{guesser passing}) = .3829 \qquad P(\text{knower failing}) = .0001$$

Clearly the two are not comparable; this task (getting 6 or more correct answers) is far too easy for the guesser.

2. Is a Score of 13 an Appropriate Cutting Point?

Guesser: $P(13 \text{ or more}) = .0002 = P(\text{passing})$
Knower: $P(13 \text{ or more}) = .7722 = P(\text{passing})$

$$1 - .7722 = .2278 = P(\text{knower failing})$$

These two figures, .0001 and .2278, are closer than the figures for the previous task, but this task is too hard for the knower.

3. Is a Score of 8 an Appropriate Cutting Point?

Guesser: $P(8$ or more$) = .1019 = P$ (passing)
Knower: $P(8$ or more$) = .9987 = P$(passing)

$$1 - .9987 = .0013 = P(\text{knower failing})$$

These figures, .1019 and .0013, are closer than for the previous task, but this task is again too easy for the guesser.

4. Is a Score of 11 an Appropriate Cutting Point?

Guesser: $P(11$ or more$) = .0040 = P$(passing)
Knower: $P(11$ or more$) = .9520 = P$(passing)

$$1 - .9520 = .0480 = P(\text{knower failing})$$

We're getting there. Let's try 10.

5. Is a Score of 10 an Appropriate Cutting Point?

Guesser: $P(10$ or more$) = .0139 = P$(passing)
Knower: $P(10$ or more$) = .9828 = P$(passing)

$$1 - .9828 = .0172 = P(\text{knower failing})$$

We won't come any closer than this. (For a cutting point of 9 the probabilities of guesser passing and knower failing are .0410 and .0052, respectively.)

Thus the "fairest" procedure is to require 10 or more correct answers.[4] For this task, the guesser has only about a 1 percent chance of success and the knower has about a 2 percent chance of failure.

But now consider the practical application of this rule after the test has been administered. Suppose a student gets fewer than 10 correct answers. Since he falls below the cutting point he will be labeled as a guesser. But there is a chance (2 percent chance) that he is really a knower who, "on a bad day," perhaps, didn't get his "usual" 70 percent or more correct. On the other hand, suppose that another student gets 10 or more cor-

---

[4] Actually the very best cutting point would be something like 9.8 correct answers, but how can a student get .8 of a question right?

rect answers. Since he falls above the cutting point he will be labeled as a knower. But there is again a chance (a 1 percent chance) that he is really a guesser who, "on a good day," just happened to guess his way to a respectable score. In each of these cases a wrong decision, an error, has been made, and the following diagram displays the kinds of errors involved:

Decision

		Student is a guesser	Student is a knower
Reality	Student is a guesser	no error ($P = .99$)	type I error ($P = .01$)
	Student is a knower	type II error ($P = .02$)	no error ($P = .98$)

Traditionally, errors of the kind wherein statements such as "the student is guessing" (such statements are called *null hypotheses*) are incorrectly rejected are called type I errors, and errors of the kind wherein other statements such as "the student is a knower" (such statements are called *alternative hypotheses*) are incorrectly rejected are called type II errors. That is,

Type I error = rejecting true null hypothesis
Type II error = rejecting true alternative hypothesis
= accepting false null hypothesis

The probability of making a type I error, that is, the probability of rejecting a true null hypothesis, is called the *level of significance*, and is usually denoted by the Greek letter α. In our example $\alpha = .01$.

The probability of making a type II error—the probability of accepting a false null hypothesis, is usually denoted by the Greek letter β. In our example, $\beta = .02$. The quantity $1 - \beta$, which is the probability of correctly establishing the hypothesis alternative to the null hypothesis (the objective of most statistical investigations) is called the *power* of the test. In our example, $1 - \beta = .98$.

chapter 3

Basic Statistical
Concepts

In the chapters on validity, reliability, and objectivity, which constitute the major portion of this book, the terms mean, variance, and correlation coefficient appear throughout. In preparation for those chapters, the following discussion of basic statistical concepts is presented.

A. ROSTER

The starting point in any statistical investigation is the raw data. The data are typically displayed in a rectangular array, called a *roster*, with the names or code letters or identification numbers of the individuals, or "subjects" of the investigation, written down the left-hand side, the names or numbers of the tests, or *variables*, written along the top, and the actual data, or scores, comprising the body of the table.

Table 1 is an example of a roster of scores obtained by 45 individuals on three tests given in a course in psychological statistics which I recently taught.

B. FREQUENCY DISTRIBUTION

If the number of individuals is quite large, say 30 or more, it is very difficult to look at the roster and make any sense out of it. A first step in bringing order out of chaos is to arrange in order of magnitude the scores obtained by the subjects on each of the variables, grouping together scores of equal or near-equal magnitude and counting them. This process is referred to as the construction of a *frequency distribution.*

Table 2 is a frequency distribution of the scores on the first hour examination.

The number of score intervals and the size of the interval

TABLE 1
ROSTER OF SCORES ON THREE EXAMINA-
TIONS IN PSYCHOLOGICAL STATISTICS

Individual	First Hour Examination	Second Hour Examination	Final Examination
A	47	78	70
B	66	83	63
C	68	67	84
D	70	66	73
E	57	65	84
F	56	64	83
G	60	69	77
H	54	78	61
I	63	96	80
J	48	41	77
K	51	67	75
L	88	86	92
M	64	90	69
N	62	60	75
O	61	82	73
P	75	82	82
Q	69	79	78
R	82	86	81
S	80	89	82
T	58	75	72
U	75	59	86
V	71	72	70
W	57	68	68
X	92	83	93
Y	62	51	72
Z	49	59	76
AA	63	71	75
BB	72	72	84
CC	83	91	83
DD	67	75	79
EE	58	39	67
FF	34	13	50
GG	49	79	64
HH	73	59	71
II	73	80	74
JJ	55	54	77
KK	55	82	72
LL	58	87	73
MM	76	76	64
NN	79	76	85
OO	56	39	66
PP	74	69	72
QQ	81	70	83
RR	61	88	73
SS	61	40	69

TABLE 2
FREQUENCY DISTRIBUTION OF SCORES ON
THE FIRST HOUR EXAMINATION

Score	Tally	Frequency
30-39	1	1
40-49	1111	4
50-59	11111111111	11
60-69	1111111111111	13
70-79	1111111111	10
80-89	11111	5
90-99	1	1
		45

are arbitrary but should be chosen so as to give as clear as possible a picture of the essential information contained in the
data. I hold no particular brief for the number and size of intervals that I chose, other than to point out that many fewer than
seven intervals would tend to eclipse the variability among the
scores, whereas many more than seven intervals would tend to
overmagnify the variability in the form of a rather anemic-look-
ing distribution with small frequencies throughout, thereby
representing little improvement over the list of scores contained
in the roster itself.

Although the frequency distribution has the disadvantage
of sacrificing the actual magnitude of each score in favor of
score intervals, it has the advantages of:

1. ordering of the scores (in our example, from a low in the
   30's to a high somewhere in the 90's)
2. grouping-together of the scores (in our example we know
   how many individuals scored in the 30's, how many
   scored in the 40's, etc.)
3. conveying a picture of the concentration of the scores
   (in our example most of the scores are concentrated in
   the 50's, 60's, and 70's, with very few low scores and
   very few high scores)

If the score intervals are arranged from lowest to highest, as
in the above example (this choice is also arbitrary), and you
rotate your paper 90 degrees counterclockwise, the "tally" section of the frequency distribution becomes a *histogram*, which
is a graphical representation of the distribution of the scores.

Tables 3 and 4 are the frequency distributions of the scores on the second hour examination and the final examination, respectively. In Table 3 I used the same size interval as in Table 2 (10 points), but there were more intervals since the scores had a wider range. In Table 4 I used a 5-point interval.

TABLE 3
FREQUENCY DISTRIBUTION OF SCORES ON
THE SECOND HOUR EXAMINATION

Score	Tally	Frequency
10-19	1	1
20-29		0
30-39	11	2
40-49	11	2
50-59	11111	5
60-69	111111111	9
70-79	111111111111	12
80-89	11111111111	11
90-99	111	3
		45

TABLE 4
FREQUENCY DISTRIBUTION OF SCORES ON
THE FINAL EXAMINATION

Score	Tally	Frequency
50-54	1	1
55-59		0
60-64	1111	4
65-69	11111	5
70-74	111111111111	12
75-79	111111111	9
80-84	1111111111	10
85-89	11	2
90-94	11	2
		45

C. MEAN

After a frequency distribution has been prepared, it is of interest to summarize the data even more by calculating some measure of the "typical" performance on each of the tests, that is, one number that will best represent the performance of the group under investigation. There are many candidates for this measure, and most statistics textbooks delve deeply into the relative merits and demerits of each (see for example, Hays, 1963). But the one measure which seems to be most relevant for educational tests is the *mean* (technically the *arithmetic mean*, since there are also geometric means and harmonic means), or familiar "average" obtained by adding up the scores and dividing by the number of scores. This can be expressed in symbols as

$$\text{mean} = M = \frac{\Sigma X}{N} \tag{3-1}$$

where the symbol Σ is read "add up" or "the sum of," X stands for any score, and N is the number of individuals in the group. I will occasionally use a subscript with the M, if there is any ambiguity concerning which scores are being considered. For example, if I am referring to two tests X and Y, I shall use the symbol M_X to denote the mean of the X-scores and M_Y to denote the mean of the Y-scores. The formula for M_Y is $\frac{\Sigma Y}{N}$. For the roster of scores listed above, the mean of the scores on the first hour examination, for example, is equal to $\frac{2913}{45} = 64.7$. (When working with raw scores which are integers, it is conventional to report the mean to one or two decimal places.)

The mean score on the second hour examination is 70.1 and the mean score on the final examination is 75.1.

The mean is a statistic which is directly analogous to the concept of center-of-gravity in physical science. If the scores on the first hour examination were to be thought of as weights hung at distances measured from the left end of a plank of wood, the fulcrum of the plank would be located at a distance of 64.7 units from the left end of the plank.

The mean is not the score that was obtained by more individuals than any other score (that's the *mode*), nor the score which is located in the center of the distribution with an equal number of scores above it and below it (that's the *median*).[1] It is merely the average score in this very special center-of-gravity sense.

---

[1] For certain distributions the mean may be equal to the mode or the median. For the normal distribution (see p. 37) all three are equal.

D. VARIANCE AND STANDARD DEVIATION

In addition to a measure of the average performance on a test, we are often interested in a measure of the variability, or dispersion, or spread, of the scores on the test. We could have one distribution of scores with a mean of 50, say, with every score exactly equal to 50, and another distribution also with a mean of 50, but with no score equal to 50 (e.g., half of the scores could be equal to 20 and the other half equal to 80). Clearly we want to be able to distinguish between two such distributions.

Again, there are several candidates for measures of variability, and the advantages and disadvantages of each are spelled out in standard texts in statistics (see Hays, 1963). The measures most commonly employed in the evaluation of educational tests are the *variance*, which is the average squared difference, or deviation, from the mean, and the *standard deviation*, which is the square root of the variance:

$$\text{variance} = \frac{\Sigma \ (X - M)^2}{N} \tag{3-2}$$

$$\text{standard deviation} = \sqrt{\frac{\Sigma \ (X - M)^2}{N}} \tag{3-3}$$

where Σ, X, M, and N are as defined before.

Since the variance and the standard deviation are functionally related one to the other (standard deviation = square root of variance; variance = square of standard deviation) they really represent a single measure of the variability of a set of scores, viz., a measure of how closely the scores are clustered around the mean of the distribution. If most of the scores are very near the mean, $X - M$ will be small for most individuals, its square will be small, the sum of these squares will be small, and upon division by N we will get a small number. If most of the scores are far from the mean, $X - M$ will be large, so will its square and their sum, and upon division by N we will get a large number.

There are several reasons for having both measures, however. For one thing, the variance comes out in squared units, rather than in the original units of measurement, and the extraction of the square root puts us back in the proper units. Secondly, the variance has interesting combinatorial properties, important in advanced statistics, which the standard deviation fails to possess. Finally, the standard deviation is related very closely to standard scores and to the normal distribution, two very important concepts which are treated later in this chapter.

Since we will need symbols for these two quantities for subsequent work, we have our choice of using V for variance, and $\sqrt{V}$ for standard deviation; or using S for standard deviation, and S^2 for variance. In line with statistical tradition we shall adopt the latter symbolism, since we shall want to focus the greater part of our attention on the standard deviation. (Subscripts on the S will be used whenever there is any doubt as to the variable under consideration.)

For the scores on the first hour examination listed in the above roster, $\Sigma (X - M)^2 = 6354.90$ and $N = 45$; thus the variance $= S^2 = \dfrac{6354.90}{45} = 141.22$. The standard deviation $= S = \sqrt{141.22} = 11.9$. (It is conventional to report the variance to two decimal places and the standard deviation to one or two.)

The variances and standard deviations of the other two tests are as follows:

Second Hour Examination	Final Examination
$S^2 = 275.25$	$S^2 = 67.95$
$S = 16.6$	$S = 8.2$

As shown in the Appendix (p. 77), the standard deviation is associated with the *range* of the scores (the range is merely the difference between the highest and the lowest score) as

$$\text{minimum value of } S = \frac{\text{range}}{\sqrt{2N}} \tag{3-4}$$

$$\text{maximum value of } S = \frac{\text{range}}{2} \tag{3-5}$$

These results hold regardless of the distribution of the scores, and thus provide an approximate check on the computation of the standard deviation. For example, for the first hour examination scores, the range $= 92 - 34 = 58$. $\dfrac{58}{\sqrt{2\,(45)}} = \dfrac{58}{\sqrt{90}} = \dfrac{58}{9.5} = 6.1$; $58/2 = 29$. Thus the standard deviation must lie somewhere between 6.1 and 29. Had we made an error in the accumulation of the sum of squares, or in the extraction of the square root, or in any of the other operations involved in the calculation of the standard deviation, and obtained an answer of 41.3, say, knowing the above relationships we would know that this must be wrong; otherwise the error might go undetected. Even with this partial check, however, there is no substitute for repeating the calculation. Smaller, less flagrant errors can still be made.

E. STANDARD SCORE

Actual "raw" scores are very difficult to interpret. Knowing only that individual A got a score of 47 on the first hour examination, we know very little. Why? First of all, we don't know what the maximum possible score that he could have gotten is. But even knowing that (it happened to be 100 in this case) and having converted the raw score into a percent-of-possible score, we still don't know very much. A raw score of 47 corresponds to 47 percent for this test. Our first reaction is that this is a pretty poor performance, since we are so used to thinking in terms of 60, 65, or 70 percent of possible as minimum passing scores. But the test may have been very difficult for all of the students, and a score of 47 percent may not really be as bad as it may first seem to be.

The upshot of all of this is that in order to be able to intelligently interpret a score on a test we need to know more than just the raw score itself and its percent-of-possible equivalent. A *standard score* is a type of score which provides us with most of the information about an individual's performance which we need for an appropriate appraisal. Standard score is defined as

$$\text{standard score} = z = \frac{X - M}{S} \tag{3-6}$$

where X = the individual's raw score, M = the mean of the raw scores, and S = the standard deviation of the raw scores.

For example, individual A's standard score on the first hour examination is obtained as

$$z = \frac{47 - 64.7}{11.9} = \frac{-17.7}{11.9} = -1.49$$

(It is conventional to report standard scores to two decimal places.)

A's standard score provides us with two pieces of information which his raw score did not. The minus sign tells us that his score was below the mean; the magnitude of the score tells us that he was 1.49 standard deviation units below the mean. Since one standard deviation is usually about one-fifth of the range, a score that is 1.49 standard deviations below the mean is well down toward the bottom of the distribution.

A standard score is thus a measure of how far from the mean any given raw score is, in terms of the standard deviation of the raw scores. Standard scores are "dimensionless"; they do not depend on the units of measurement as do the raw scores, since division of $X - M$, which has dimension, by S, which has the same dimension, removes the unit of measurement from consideration. In the Appendix (p. 79) I show that the mean of any set of standard scores is equal to zero, and the variance and standard deviation are both equal to one. Therefore the transformation of raw scores to standard scores provides a new set of scores which have very desirable statistical properties.

A complete roster of standard score equivalents to the raw scores of Table 1 is given in Table 5.

F. PEARSON PRODUCT-MOMENT CORRELATION COEFFICIENT

Up to this point our discussion has been concerned with describing or summarizing the data *one variable at a time*. We considered the mean, variance, and standard deviation of the scores on the first hour examination, the second hour examination, and the final examination independently of one another. It is of both theoretical and practical interest to also consider the *relationships* among variables. We would like to know, for example, if individuals who get high scores on the first exam tend also to get high scores on the second exam, or if individuals who get high scores on the first exam tend to get low scores on the second exam, or if there is little relationship between scores on the first exam and scores on the second exam.

Once more, there are several ways we can measure the relationship between variables (see Hays, 1963), depending upon the nature of the data, but the appropriate measure for most

TABLE 5
STANDARD(z) SCORES ON THREE EXAMINATIONS IN PSYCHOLOGICAL STATISTICS

Individual	First Hour Examination	Second Hour Examination	Final Examination
A	−1.49	.48	−.62
B	.11	.78	−1.48
C	.28	−.19	1.09
D	.45	−.25	−.26
E	−.65	−.31	1.09
F	−.73	−.37	.96
G	−.39	−.07	.23
H	−.90	.48	−1.72
I	−.14	1.56	.60
J	−1.40	−1.75	.23
K	−1.15	−.19	−.01
L	1.96	.96	2.06
M	−.06	1.20	−.74
N	−.23	−.61	−.01
O	−.31	.72	−.26
P	.87	.72	.84
Q	.36	.54	.35
R	1.45	.96	.72
S	1.29	1.14	.84
T	−.56	.30	−.38
U	.87	−.67	1.33
V	.53	.11	−.62
W	−.65	−.13	−.87
X	2.29	.78	2.18
Y	−.23	−1.15	−.38
Z	−1.32	−.67	.11
AA	−.14	.05	−.01
BB	.61	.11	1.09
CC	1.54	1.26	.96
DD	.19	.30	.48
EE	−.56	−1.87	−.99
FF	−2.58	−3.44	−3.06
GG	−1.32	.54	−1.35
HH	.70	−.67	−.50
II	.70	.60	−.13
JJ	−.82	−.97	.23
KK	−.82	.72	−.38
LL	−.56	1.02	−.26
MM	.95	.36	−1.35
NN	1.20	.36	1.21
OO	−.73	−1.87	−1.11
PP	.78	−.07	−.38
QQ	1.37	−.01	.96
RR	−.31	1.08	−.26
SS	−.31	−1.81	−.74

educational tests is the *Pearson product-moment correlation coefficient*, which is the average product of standard score on variable X and standard score on variable Y; that is,

$$\text{Pearson product-moment correlation coefficient} = r_{XY} = \frac{\Sigma\, z_X z_Y}{N}$$

$$(3\text{-}7)$$

where z_X is an individual's standard score on variable X, z_Y is his standard score on variable Y, and N is the number of individuals in the group.

This statistic gets its name from Karl Pearson, famous British statistician who first derived it. The word "product-moment" comes from the formula itself, since what is involved is the determination of an average product, and the concept of average is related to the physical concept of finding a moment. (The mean, or center of gravity, is often called the first moment of a distribution.) The word "correlation" indicates relationship, and the word "coefficient" indicates a summary measure. The symbol r with the subscripts X and Y stands for "relationship" between X and Y. Throughout the remainder of this book I shall often refer to this statistic merely as "the correlation coefficient" or even "the correlation," for the sake of brevity, and if it is clear from the context what two variables are being correlated I shall also drop the subscripts on the r.

Since the product-moment correlation coefficient is so important and so frequently encountered in the literature of educational measurement, statistics, and research I should like to go through the underlying rationale and the mathematical derivation of this particular statistic in order to demonstrate that its formula is based on sound logic and was not just pulled out of a hat. A complete understanding of the derivation requires some background in trigonometry, analytic geometry, and differential calculus, so do not be discouraged if you cannot follow it completely. But if you persevere I am sure that you will be able to understand more than you thought you would be able to.

If we want to investigate the relationship between any two things X and Y, a good starting point is to make a two-dimensional plot of the various values of X and the corresponding values of Y. But in order to get the truest picture of the relationship between the two variables it would be better to get rid of the units of measurement. For example, if X were weight and Y were height, if we were to plot actual height against actual weight we would be plotting inches against pounds, say, and the mere choice of units might give us a distorted picture of the relationship. One way to remove the units from consideration is to convert both X and Y into standard scores and plot z_Y against z_X. If we were to do this for the scores on the first hour examination, call them X, and the scores on the second hour examination, call them Y, we would get a plot of 45 points (one point for each individual in the group) of z_Y vs. z_X (Figure 1).

The points A, B, and C correspond to individuals A, B, and C in the roster. The other points correspond to the rest of the individuals, but they have not been labeled since it would clutter up the diagram. From Table 5, individual A has a standard score of -1.49 on X and a standard score of $.48$ on Y, and the point A with coordinates -1.49 and $.48$ is plotted in the conventional manner. Points B, C, and the remaining points are determined in like manner.

In devising a measure of relationship between X and Y we must decide on *what kind* of relationship we are going to investigate. The simplest kind, the kind to which Pearson confined his investigation, is *linear* relationship. He asked the question: how close do these points come to falling on a straight line? He could have asked the same question about a parabola or an exponential function or any number of different curves. But his interest was, and our interest will be, in the linear case.

For the present example we can tell by looking at the plot of points that they do not fall on a straight line, and thus the degree of linear relationship between X and Y is not perfect. However, there is a general linear "trend" or "pattern" to the points, with most of the points in the upper-right and lower-left sections (quadrants) of the diagram, so that although they do not fall exactly on a straight line we can visualize a "best-fitting" straight line that goes through the heart of this swarm of points. The determination of this line of best fit is the crucial step in the derivation that is to follow.

In addition to restricting himself to linear relationship, Pearson also imposed a couple of other restrictions:

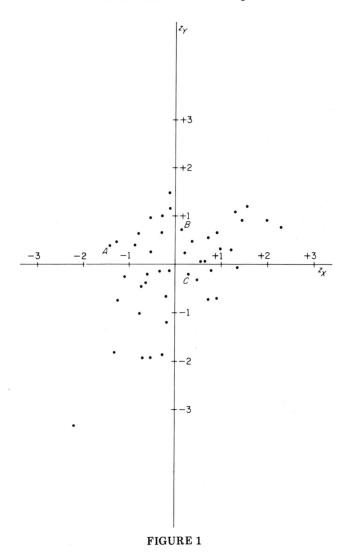

FIGURE 1

1. The line must go through the origin.
2. The criterion of "best fit" is the least-squares criterion, with the data treated in the context of a prediction, or "regression," problem wherein Y is to be predicted from X. (Since the example under consideration involves

the relationship between scores on a first test, X, and scores on a second test, Y, the casting of the problem of relationship within the framework of the problem of predicting Y from X is not only acceptable but natural.)

What line best fits these points? There is an infinite number of straight lines which pass through the origin, all of which have equation $z_Y = mz_X$, where m is the slope of the line, which by definition is the tangent of the angle that the line makes with the positive direction of the horizontal (z_X) axis. Our task is to find the line that has the particular value of m that "does the job," that is, best fits the points. This value of m will be the co-efficient of correlation between X and Y.

We could tackle the problem geometrically by trial and error, trying different lines and picking out the one which by visual inspection best fits the points. But the problem is handled more easily and accurately by analytic, or algebraic, methods, as follows.

Let $z'_Y = mz_X$ be the equation of the line for predicting Y from X. (I use z'_Y rather than z_Y to distinguish between the actual z_Y that the individual obtained and the predicted z_Y that he would have obtained were there perfect linear relationship between the variables.) Since we want the predictions to be as good as possible, we would like the z'_Y and the z_Y to be as close together as possible, and the least-squares criterion for this re-sult is that $\Sigma (z_Y - z'_Y)^2$ be a minimum, where the summation is over all of the individuals in the group.

Using C, for criterion, to denote this sum, and recalling that our task is to solve for m, we have

$$
\begin{aligned}
C &= \Sigma (z_Y - z'_Y)^2 \\
&= \Sigma (z_Y - mz_X)^2 \quad \text{(since } z'_Y = mz_X\text{)} \\
&= \Sigma (z_Y^2 - 2\,mz_Xz_Y + m^2 z_X^2) \quad \text{(by expansion)} \\
&= \Sigma z_Y^2 - 2m \Sigma z_Xz_Y + m^2 \Sigma z_X^2 \quad \text{(by Formulas A-1 and} \\
& \hspace{8.5cm} \text{A-2 of the Appendix)}
\end{aligned}
$$

By the techniques of differential calculus,

$$
\frac{dC}{dm} = -2\Sigma z_Xz_Y + (2\Sigma z_X^2)\, m
$$

Setting $\dfrac{dC}{dm} = 0$, we have

$$(2 \Sigma z_X^2) m - 2\Sigma z_X z_Y = 0$$

or

$$m = \frac{\Sigma z_X z_Y}{\Sigma z_X^2}$$

But by formula A-4 of the Appendix, $\Sigma z_X^2 = N$. Therefore

$$m = \frac{\Sigma z_X z_Y}{N}$$

and rather than use the notation m we shall use the notation r_{XY}, giving us

$$r_{XY} = \frac{\Sigma z_X z_Y}{N}$$

Thus the Pearson product-moment correlation coefficient, which is a measure of the degree of linear relationship between two variables X and Y, is equal to the slope of the line which best fits, in the least-squares sense, the plot of points z_Y against z_X.

If $z_Y = z_X$ for all individuals, all of the points will lie exactly on a straight line from lower left to upper right, i.e.,

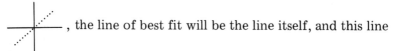

, the line of best fit will be the line itself, and this line

will make an angle of 45 degrees with the positive direction of the z_X-axis. The tangent of 45 degrees is 1, and thus $m = r = 1$. This is the case of *perfect, positive, direct* relationship between the two variables.

If $z_Y = - z_X$ for all individuals, all of the points will lie on a

straight line from lower right to upper left, i.e., ⟍⟋ , and

the line of best fit is the line itself, which makes an angle of 135 degrees with the positive direction of the z_X-axis. The tangent of 135 degrees is -1, and thus $m = r = -1$. This is the case of *perfect, negative, inverse* relationship between the two variables.

If the points comprise a "buckshot" pattern, i.e., ―――――⊞――――― ,

the line of best fit is the z_X-axis itself, which makes an angle of 0 degrees with the positive direction of the z_x-axis. The tangent of 0 degrees is 0, and thus $m = r = 0$. This is the case of zero relationship between the variables.

Therefore, r can take on the values 1, -1, 0, and any value in between 1 and -1. If the general orientation of the points is from lower left to upper right, r will be between 0 and 1 (positive relationship), whereas if the general orientation of the points is from lower right to upper left, r will be between -1 and 0 (negative relationship).

Using the data of Table 5, the correlation between scores on the first hour exam and scores on the second hour exam is equal to $\frac{22.6}{45}$ = .50. (It is conventional to report correlation coefficients to two decimal places.) These two variables are thus positively related in that individuals who scored high on the first hour exam tended to score high on the second exam, and individuals who scored low on the first hour exam tended to score low on the second exam; but the relationship is far from perfect, since there are some notable exceptions to this general tendency, e.g., individual A who scored well *below* the mean on the first exam and about half a standard deviation *above* the mean on the second exam.

The correlation between scores on the first exam and scores on the final exam is .64 and the correlation between scores on the second exam and scores on the final exam is .39.

As almost all research textbooks so wisely caution the reader, correlation is not to be identified with cause and effect. If two variables are positively related we cannot say that an individual's high score on one variable "caused" him to score high on the other variable, even if the time sequence of the two scores goes in the right direction. Both scores could have been "caused" by a high score on some third variable which has not even been taken into account.

G. THE NORMAL DISTRIBUTION

The frequency distributions of many educational and psychological variables are such that most of the scores are very close to the mean, with the remaining scores "tailing off" toward the high and low ends of the distribution in symmetric fashion, as illustrated by the histogram of Figure 2, which depicts the

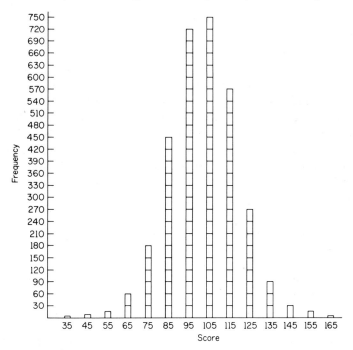

FIGURE 2. Distribution of 3184 IQ scores on the 1937 Stanford-Binet test. [Adapted from the data contained in the manual for the third revision of the Stanford-Binet Intelligence Scale (Terman & Merrill, 1960). The scores of 35, 45, . . . are the midpoints of the intervals 30-40, 40-50, . . . respectively.]

distribution of Stanford-Binet intelligence test scores for the population of individuals on which the 1937 revision was standardized (the current version is the 1960 revision). If we were to draw a smooth curve over the tops of the bars of this histogram we would obtain a picture very similar to that of Figure 3, which is the graph of the very famous normal curve so thoroughly investigated by the mathematician Carl Friedrich

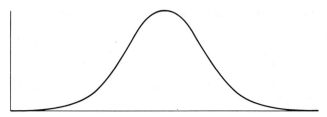

FIGURE 3. The normal curve.

Gauss (the curve is also called the Gaussian curve). The normal curve is a theoretical frequency distribution which has a complicated mathematical expression, but it has the very important property that the percentage of scores falling between any two points in the distribution can be perfectly determined if you know the mean and the standard deviation. These percentages have been tabulated for various key points. It is well known, for example, that the percentage of scores in any normal distribution lying between the point corresponding to a score of one standard deviation below the mean ($z = -1$) and the point corresponding to a score of one standard deviation above the mean ($z = 1$) is approximately 68 percent, and that the percentage of scores lying between the point corresponding to a score of two standard deviations below the mean ($z = -2$) and the point corresponding to a score of two standard deviations above the mean ($z = 2$) is approximately 95 percent. Other percentages can be determined by referring to standard normal curve tables found in any statistics text, such as Hays (1963).

The important thing about all of this is that if we either know or can assume that the distribution of scores with which we are concerned is normal or very close to normal, we can make valuable interpretations concerning relative scores on educational and psychological tests. This property is of special importance in conjunction with the reliability of tests, where the assumption of normality for the distribution of "obtained" scores around "true" scores is crucial to the theory.

chapter 4

Objectivity

A. INTRODUCTION

As I stated in Chapter 1, the criteria for a good test are validity, reliability, objectivity, and practicability. The first three characteristics are technical characteristics, and an investigation of the extent to which a given test possesses each of these properties invariably involves statistical reasoning and statistical calculations. Objectivity is treated in this chapter, reliability in Chapter 5, and validity in Chapter 6. They are taken up in this order because a test must be objective in order to be reliable (if two scorers cannot agree on the score to be assigned to a student's first performance we do not have a single score with which we can compare a subsequent performance), and a test must be reliable in order to be valid (if the scores on the two performances are not comparable we do not have a single score to use to compare with the student's performance on some external criterion).

The property of objectivity is concerned with the *scoring* of a test. A test is said to be perfectly objective if the rescoring of a set of test papers produces scores identical to the initial scores assigned to those same papers. If rescoring yields scores which bear no relationship to the original scores, the scoring of the test is not objective but subjective, completely dependent upon the judgment of the individual scorers. A thorough evaluation of any educational test must include an investigation of the degree of objectivity of the test.

The second scoring may be carried out by the same individual who did the initial scoring, in which case the property of concern is *intra*individual objectivity. More commonly the second scoring is performed by a different individual (typically a professional colleague), in which case the property of concern is *inter*individual objectivity. And of course the process can be generalized to more than two scorings by the same individual or to repeated scorings by more than two different individuals.

Rescoring may produce scores which are different in score level but which are perfectly correlated with the original scores. For example, a second reading, by a second reader, of a set of history papers may result in scores which are uniformly ten points higher than the scores assigned by the first reader, but with the individuals in the same rank-order. (The second reader may be "an easy marker" or the first reader "a hard marker," with the two agreeing perfectly on *relative* performances.) Although technically a test for which this sort of thing happens should be labeled subjective, I prefer to call it objective, for rescoring does not destroy the relative order of performance of the individuals taking the test. It is the *relationship* between scores that is of prime concern.

Most standardized tests consist entirely of true-false, multiple-choice, or matching items, and have near-perfect objectivity (which is the reason why they are called objective tests), since once the scoring key has been determined, scoring and rescoring are mechanical operations (often actually done by machines) which obviate personal judgments.[1]

But tests that contain open-ended items (completion, short-answer, essay) require the scorer to rule upon the "rightness" or "wrongness" of each response, since no matter how complete the scoring key may appear, responses will be given which have not been anticipated. The remarks that follow and the statistical procedures that are described pertain to the evaluation of educational tests which are either wholly or partially open-ended.

B. STATISTICAL TECHNIQUES FOR INVESTIGATING OBJECTIVITY

All of the methods for determining the degree of objectivity of a test are concerned with the correlation between the first-reading and the second-reading scores. But the coefficient used as a measure of the amount of relationship between the two sets of scores varies according to the type of "scale" (measuring instrument) employed and the number of papers being scored.

---

[1] Objectivity is near-perfect rather than perfect since one must allow for occasional clerical errors in the use of the scoring key. Even test-scoring machines can be "off" by a full point or more on a damp day!

1. Interval Scale and Large Numbers of Papers

If the data conform to the requirements of an *interval scale* (ordered values with a unit which is constant throughout the scale)[2] and the number of papers is large, the Pearson product-moment correlation coefficient (Chapter 3, p. 29) is the statistic most often employed. An example from Jackson (1940) will illustrate the use of this statistic in determining the degree of objectivity of a test. One section of a particular test with which he was concerned had no scoring key, the marking of that section being left completely to the judgment of the individual scorers. The question arose as to whether the error introduced was large enough to justify changing the form of that part of the test or constructing an elaborate key. Twenty papers were chosen at random from a set of papers and were marked independently by two examiners—call them X and Y. The scores were as follows.[3]

Individual	Scores assigned by examiners	
	X	Y
1	18	19
2	20	20
3	30	31
4	17	19
5	24	22
6	33	36
7	21	22
8	16	18
9	33	35
10	24	26
11	12	14
12	16	16
13	23	24
14	25	28
15	30	32
16	22	25
17	24	28
18	27	27
19	27	31
20	31	31

[2] For a thorough treatment of nominal, ordinal, interval, and ratio scales see Hays (1963).

[3] Jackson's example actually involved *three* independent examiners but I have selected two of the sets of scores in order to illustrate this particular technique.

Transforming the raw scores to standard scores and substituting these values into the formula for the Pearson product-moment correlation coefficient (3-7), we find that r_{XY} = .95. Thus the two examiners were in very close agreement as to the relative merit of each paper. There seemed to be a systematic difference in the severity of the examiners, however, with M_X = 23.7 and M_Y = 25.2. It was decided that a scoring guide should be constructed which would tend to reduce the difference between examiners, but that it was not necessary to change the form of the items which comprised that section of the test.

2. Interval Scale and Small Numbers of Papers

If we have an interval scale and the number of papers is small the Pearson product-moment correlation coefficient may still be used, but a common procedure is to sacrifice some sensitivity contained in the actual data by having the papers merely put in rank-order (according to scale value) at each scoring and computing the *Spearman rank-difference correlation coefficient* r_S for the two rankings. (The subscript S is for Spearman, another famous British statistician.) This coefficient is identical to the product-moment correlation coefficient obtaining between rankings, but the formula is somewhat simpler:

$$r_S = 1 - \frac{6\Sigma d^2}{N^3 - N} \qquad (4\text{-}1)$$

where d is the difference between the rankings for each individual and N is the number of individuals ranked.

If the two sets of rankings are identical, $d = 0$ for each individual, $d^2 = 0, \Sigma d^2 = 0$, and $r_S = 1$. If one ranking is the complete reverse of the other (e.g., 12345 vs. 54321) it turns out that $\Sigma d^2 = \dfrac{N^3 - N}{3}$ and $r_S = -1$. This is not surprising, since the product-moment correlation coefficient possesses this property and, as pointed out above, $r_S = r_{XY}$ when X and Y both consist of ranks from 1 to N. The use of this statistic in investigating test objectivity, including the procedure for dealing with "ties," is illustrated in the treatment of the data atop page 43 which has been taken from Thorndike and Hagen (1955).

Since individual F received the highest score, 99, at the first reading, he is assigned rank 1 for that reading. Individuals C, D, E, and J all got the same next-highest score, 90, and are

Individual	Score assigned at first reading (X)	Score assigned at second reading two months later by same reader (Y)
A	85	70
B	50	75
C	90	95
D	90	85
E	90	70
F	99	90
G	70	60
H	75	80
I	60	80
J	90	75

therefore tied for ranks 2, 3, 4, and 5. When ties occur the procedure almost universally adopted is to assign to each individual the average (mean) of the ranks for which they are tied. Individuals C, D, E, and J are therefore all given rank 3.5. Individual A, with a score of 85, gets rank 6; individual H rank 7; individual G rank 8; individual I rank 9; and individual B rank 10.

The second-reading scores are similarly ranked. Three ties occur, for ranks 4 and 5, for ranks 6 and 7, and for ranks 8 and 9, and they are resolved as before.

The two rankings, the differences between the rankings, and the squares of these differences are:

Individual	Rank at first reading	Rank at second reading	d	d^2
A	6	8.5	-2.5	6.25
B	10	6.5	3.5	12.25
C	3.5	1	2.5	6.25
D	3.5	3	.5	.25
E	3.5	8.5	-5	25
F	1	2	-1	1
G	8	10	-2	4
H	7	4.5	2.5	6.25
I	9	4.5	4.5	20.25
J	3.5	6.5	-3	9

From this table[4] we find that $\Sigma d^2 = 90.50$, and with $N^3 - N = 10^3 - 10 = 990$, Formula 4-1 gives $r_S = .45$. The relationship between the two rankings is direct but certainly not

[4] As a check on the accuracy of the computation note that $\Sigma d = 0$. This must always be the case regardless of the degree of relationship between the ranks.

very impressive when one considers that this is a case of *intra*-individual agreement, the same individual doing the scoring on two different occasions. And as Thorndike and Hagen point out, if these data were used for assigning grades in the percent-of-possible grading system, with 65 percent of possible the minimum passing point, the two individuals (B and I) who "failed" at the first reading would "pass" at second reading while individual G, who "passed" at first reading, would "fail" at second reading.

The product-moment correlation coefficient, r_{XY}, obtaining between the *actual scale values* for the two occasions is .37. Thus the sacrificing of sensitivity in the data by using ranks rather than actual scores produced an error of .08 in the correlation coefficient. Had there not been so many ties the difference would have been somewhat smaller, but the two will be equal only when the differences between the actual scores are directly proportional to the differences between the ranks.[5]

The technique of rank-correlation can also be used when one never even has any actual scale values (nor any scale for that matter) to start with, the scoring process being a ranking process from the outset. An example of a situation where ranks are the basic and only data is the judging of a beauty contest. A beauty contest is a "test" of beauty, but beauty is an attribute for which it is difficult to construct an adequate scale. Nevertheless, given a sample of N candidates it is assumed that it is possible for a judge to rank the candidates from 1 to N in order of his perception of beauty. If a second judge also ranks the same candidates, the technique of rank-correlation can be used to investigate the relationship between the two sets of rankings. Incidentally, the property under investigation in this example is also the property of *objectivity*. Educational tests are not the only kinds of "measurement" (forgive the *double entendre*) situations where objectivity is a problem.

3. Ordinal Scale and Large Numbers of Papers

If we have an *ordinal scale* (ordered values but no unit) and the number of papers is large, the appropriate measure of the de-

---

[5] There are *three* correlation coefficients involved: (1) the product-moment correlation between the actual scores; (2) the product-moment correlation between the ranks; and (3) the rank-correlation coefficient. The last two are identical when there are no ties.

gree of relationship between two readings is a coefficient derived from a *contingency table*, or "two-way" frequency distribution, which displays the relevant data as illustrated by the following example taken from Furst (1958).

Two readers have graded the same essay question for 50 students on a five-point scale. The number of students who received each combination of ratings is as follows (blank spaces in the table correspond to zero frequencies, i.e., no students received those ratings):

Score at second reading (by second reader)

		1	2	3	4	5	Row totals
	5			1	5	7	13
	4			8	7	1	16
Score at	3	1	6	7			14
first reading	2	2	3	1			6
(by first reader)	1	1					1
Column totals		4	9	17	12	8	50

If all of the frequencies were located in the diagonal from lower left to upper right there would be perfect agreement between the readers. If all of the frequencies were located in the opposite diagonal from lower right to upper left there would be perfect disagreement between the readers. (A "buckshot" pattern of frequencies would be indicative of a condition about halfway between perfect agreement and perfect disagreement— that is, a condition whereby the two sets of ratings are essentially independent.)

Because perfect objectivity depends only on *relative* and not absolute agreement, if the frequencies were all located in *any* of the lower-left to upper-right diagonals of this table there would be perfect direct relationship between the ratings, and if they were located in any of the lower-right to upper-left diagonals there would be perfect inverse relationship.

As is desirable and conventional for almost all measures of relationship, the statistic used to summarize the information contained in this type of table should take on the value 1 for perfect direct relationship and the value -1 for perfect inverse relationship, assuming intermediate values for intermediate locations of the frequencies.

The *index of order association* γ is such a statistic. This measure was developed by Goodman and Kruskal (1954), and modified by Senders (1958). It involves the comparison of each individual with every other individual with respect to whether scores assigned to the second individual exceeded those assigned to the first individual on *both* of the variables, or whether the second individual scored higher on one of the variables but lower on the other variable ("lower on both" and 'ties" may be ignored). Letting S (for *same*) denote the number of comparisons of each individual with every other individual wherein one individual exceeded the other on both variables, and D (for *different*) denote the number of comparisons wherein one individual exceeded the other on one of the variables but was exceeded by the other on the other variable, the formula for the index of order association is

$$\gamma = \frac{S - D}{S + D} \qquad (4\text{-}2)$$

If all of the comparisons are of the type whereby a higher score on one variable is always associated with a higher score on the second variable, $D = 0$ and $\gamma = \frac{S}{S} = 1$. If all of the comparisons are of the type whereby a higher score on one variable is always associated with a lower score on the second variable, $S = 0$ and $\gamma = \frac{-D}{D} = -1$.

The number of S and D comparisons is determined as follows:

1. For each "cell" (entry) of the table find the number of individuals who scored higher on both variables than the individuals in that cell. Multiply that number by the number of individuals in the cell itself. Do this for each cell in the table. Add across cells. The result is equal to S.
2. For each cell of the table find the number of individuals who score higher on one variable, but lower on the other, than the individuals in that cell. Multiply that number by the number of individuals in the cell itself. Do this for each cell of the table. Add across cells. The result is equal to D.

Consider the 1-1 cell (bottom row, first column)[6] of the table above. All but three individuals (the three other scores of 1 assigned by the second reader) scored higher on both variables than the one individual in that cell. They are the $1 + 5 + 7 = 13$ individuals in the top row, the $8 + 7 + 1 = 16$ individuals in the next row, the $6 + 7 = 13$ individuals in the next row (the one individual in the 3-1 cell scored higher on one variable but tied on the other), and the $3 + 1 = 4$ individuals in the next-to-last row (the two individuals in the 2-1 cell are not counted), a total of 46 individuals—the total of all of the frequencies *above and to the right* of the 1-1 cell. There are, then, $46 \times 1 = 46$ comparisons involving the one individual in the 1-1 cell which are S comparisons.

For the 2-1 cell there are $[(1 + 5 + 7) + (8 + 7 + 1) + (6 + 7)] \times 2 = 84$ S comparisons. The other cells are treated in like manner.

For the 1-1, 2-1, and 3-1 cells there are *no D* comparisons, since there are no frequencies at all to the left of these cells. For the 2-2 cell there is only one individual (the entry "1" in the 3-1 cell) *above and to the left*, yielding $1 \times 3 = 3$ D comparisons. For the 2-3 cell there are $(1 + 6) \times 1 = 7$ D comparisons, etc.

The computational "layout" atop page 48 is helpful for this example and for all other examples involving the use of the index of order association.

Substituting the values for S and D into Formula 4-2 gives $\gamma = .94$. The two readers are therefore in quite close agreement as to the relative merit of the 50 papers. But just as was the case for the Jackson data (see above) there is a systematic difference in the severity of the two readers. (Reader No. 1 gave twenty-nine 4's and 5's, for example, whereas Reader No. 2 gave only twenty.)

4. Ordinal Scale and Small Numbers of Papers

For ordinal scales and a small number of papers the rank-correlation procedure (Sec. 2, above) is used.

---

[6] All of the cells are designated in this fashion. The number before the hyphen refers to the row and the number after the hyphen refers to the column.

Cell	Cell frequency, f	$f \uparrow$ and $\rightarrow$	Contribution to S	$f \uparrow$ and $\leftarrow$	Contribution to D
1-1	1	46	46	0	0
2-1	2	42	84	0	0
2-2	3	36	108	1	3
2-3	1	20	20	7	7
3-1	1	29	29	0	0
3-2	6	29	174	0	0
3-3	7	20	140	0	0
4-3	8	12	96	0	0
4-4	7	7	49	1	7
4-5	1	0	0	6	6
			$S = 746$		$D = 23$

5. Scale-Type and Sample Size Problems

Unfortunately there are fine-line distinctions between interval and ordinal scales and there is no magic number above which numbers are "large" numbers and below which numbers are "small" numbers, and thus two or more of the above techniques may be equally appropriate in dealing with certain kinds of data. For example, consider the following problem taken from Wert, Neidt, and Ahmann (1954):

Two instructors independently assigned final course marks to the same class of students in beginning educational psychology. The marking system used involved marks from 1 to 9.

Individual	Instructor		Individual	Instructor	
	X	Y		X	Y
1	8	8	17	7	6
2	4	3	18	7	7
3	5	5	19	9	7
4	6	5	20	3	2
5	4	4	21	2	2
6	8	8	22	8	6
7	8	9	23	5	5
8	7	5	24	4	4
9	7	6	25	6	5
10	6	5	26	5	5
11	5	5	27	1	1
12	3	4	28	7	5
13	3	4	29	6	5
14	5	4	30	2	2
15	4	3	31	8	7
16	7	5			

The data arise from a nine-point rating scale. Some investigators consider such scales as interval scales and would go right ahead and compute the Pearson product-moment correlation coefficient. Others consider them ordinal scales and would prefer to display the data in a 9 × 9 contingency table, but are subsequently dismayed at the preponderance of small frequencies in the table.

There are 31 individuals in the sample. Is this number small enough to suggest simplifying the computations (and sacrificing some information) by ranking the individuals for each reading? Perhaps, but the trouble with this is that with 31 individuals and only nine scale values there will be a great many ties and *too much* information may be sacrificed.

The investigator must let the data themselves dictate what seems to him to be the most relevant measure of relationship. If the data are "good" data yielded by a sensitive scale with a defensible unit of measurement, the Pearson product-moment correlation coefficient should be used if at all possible since not only is it the most traditional of the measures of relationship, but it also preserves all of the information contained in the actual data. If the scale is such that the usual equal-interval assumption for the product-moment correlation coefficient is not at all tenable, one of the other procedures must be used.

chapter 5

Reliability

A. THE AXIOMATIC APPROACH TO RELIABILITY

In the study of plane geometry there are certain intuitively satisfying, unproven assertions—for example, the statements "the whole is equal to the sum of the parts" and "through a point not on a line one and only one line can be drawn parallel to the given line," some of which are called *postulates* and some of which are called *axioms*. There are also other statements, called *theorems*, which are proven using various postulates, axioms, definitions, and previously proven theorems. Every mathematical system has its axioms, which are the *assumptions* of the system, and its theorems, which are results which can be demonstrated to hold on the basis of the axioms. In this chapter I should like to treat test scores in the context of a mathematical system, deriving in this system the principal results concerning test reliability. I shall prove two of the theorems within the chapter itself, so that you can get "the feel" of this approach to test reliability. Proofs of the rest of the theorems are found in the appendix.

Axiom 1: Any individual's *obtained score* on a test (the score he actually gets) is the sum of his *true score* (the score he should have gotten) and his *error score* (a random component which accounts for the difference between his true score and his error score). That is, if X = obtained score, T = true score, and E = error score, we have

$$X = T + E$$

Since axioms are supposed to be intuitively satisfying assumptions, we should convince ourselves that this particular axiom is acceptable. An example should suffice. Johnny gets a raw score of 64 on a test. Every test consists of a small sample of all possible questions that could be asked. On this particular sample Johnny got a score of 64. If this were a 75-item test, a raw score of 64 would correspond to a percent-of-possible score of 85 percent. Perhaps he really knows only 81 percent of the answers to all of the questions that could be asked, and it just so happened that this particular sample of questions contained a slightly better-than-average number of questions to which he knew the right answers. It is a matter of chance, or luck, that he got a score of 85 percent, or 64, rather than his "true" 81 percent, or 61. The difference of 3 points is random error.

Since $X = T + E$, if X is greater than T, E will be positive; if X is less than T, E will be negative. Unfortunately we never actually know an individual's true score and thus cannot determine his error score, but we can say *something* about true and error scores, as the subsequent discussion will show.

Axiom 2: For each individual, across all administrations of all possible samples of questions that could be asked, and for any large group of individuals on any one administration of the same sample of questions, the average error score is equal to zero; i.e., $M_E = 0$.

This axiom is also intuitively satisfying, since if error scores are truly random, they should "play no favorites." If an individual happens to pick up a positive error on one administration of a test, there is no reason to believe that he should continue to pick up positive errors on subsequent administrations—that is, the errors should balance out across administrations. Similarly, for any one administration of a given sample of questions to a large group of students, the sample should be a "good" sample for some and a "bad" sample for others, so that the average difference between true and obtained score should be zero.

Theorem 1: For any given administration of a test to a large group of N individuals, the mean obtained score is equal to the mean true score; i.e., $M_X = M_T$.

Proof

By Axiom 1,

$$X = T + E$$

Therefore

$$\Sigma X = \Sigma(T + E)$$
$$= \Sigma T + \Sigma E \qquad \text{(by Formula A-2 of Appendix)}$$

Dividing through by N,

$$\frac{\Sigma X}{N} = \frac{\Sigma T}{N} + \frac{\Sigma E}{N}$$

But

$$\frac{\Sigma X}{N} = M_X, \quad \frac{\Sigma T}{N} = M_T, \quad \frac{\Sigma E}{N} = M_E$$

Therefore

$$M_X = M_T + M_E$$

But by Axiom 2,

$$M_E = 0$$

Therefore

$$M_X = M_T$$

Theorem 1 tells us that, under the assumptions of the theory as represented by Axioms 1 and 2, no matter what kind of test we have, the average obtained score that we get is equal to the average true score that we should have gotten.

Axiom 3: True scores and error scores are uncorrelated; i.e., $r_{TE} = 0$. This axiom is also very reasonable, since error scores are assumed to be random.

Theorem 2: For any given administration of a test to a large group of individuals, the variance of the obtained scores is equal to the variance of the true scores plus the variance of the error scores; that is, $S_X^2 = S_T^2 + S_E^2$. (Proof given in Appendix, p. 80.)

Theorem 2 tells us that the spread of the obtained scores is composed of the spread of the true scores and the spread of the error scores. If the test is a "good" test in the sense that the error scores are small, the variance of the errors will be small, and most of the obtained variance will be true variance. If on the other hand the test is a "bad" test in the sense that the errors are large, the variance of the errors will be large, and most of the obtained variance will be error variance.

Axiom 4: For each individual, across administrations, and for each large group of individuals on the same administration, the error scores are normally distributed with constant standard deviation S_E.

This assumption about the distribution of error scores merely asserts that small errors are more frequent than large errors, with intermediate-size errors being of intermediate frequency, and that the spread of the error scores is the same for all individuals and all administrations—i.e., that the test is equally good or equally bad for measuring each individual. For some tests the standard deviation of the error scores, commonly abbreviated to *the standard error of measurement*, may be very small, meaning that the test is quite accurate in yielding scores which are very close to true scores. For other tests the standard error of measurement may be quite large, meaning that the test is not very accurate in this respect.

Definition 1: The *reliability coefficient* of a test is the ratio of the true variance to the obtained variance; that is, using the symbol r_{XX} for reliability coefficient,

$$r_{XX} = \frac{S_T^2}{S_X^2}$$

From this definition and from Theorem 2 we can see that if the error scores are small and the variance of the error scores (S_E^2) is small, S_T^2 will be large and very close to S_X^2, so that r_{XX} will be very close to 1. In the extreme, if all of the errors are equal to zero, S_E^2 will also be equal to zero, S_T^2 will be equal to S_X^2, and r_{XX} will be equal to 1. On the other hand, if the error scores are large, S_E^2 will be large, S_T^2 will be small, and r_{XX} will be very close to 0. In the extreme, if all of the obtained variance is error variance, S_E^2 will be equal to S_X^2, S_T^2 will be equal to zero, and r_{XX} will be equal to 0. Thus, a test which yields low error scores has a high reliability coefficient, a test which yields high error scores has a low reliability coefficient. The largest value r_{XX} can take on is 1, and the smallest value that r_{XX} can take on is 0.

In the preceding paragraph I have used the notation r_{XX} for the reliability coefficient. In Chapter 3 I used the notation r_{XY} for the Pearson product-moment coefficient of correlation between any two variables X and Y. Is the reliability coefficient, which is defined as the ratio of true variance to obtained variance, also a correlation coefficient, or am I just trying to confuse you with similar notation? I am happy to say that the answer is that it *is* a correlation coefficient, but a very special kind of correlation of a test with itself (thus the notation r_{XX}), and this fact will be demonstrated in the proof of Theorem 3, which follows. But first we need another definition and another axiom.

Definition 2: Two forms A and B of a test are said to be *equivalent* or *parallel* or *alternate* if

$$T_A = T_B \quad \text{for each individual}$$

$$S_{E_A}^2 = S_{E_B}^2 \quad \begin{array}{l} \text{for each large group of individuals to} \\ \text{whom both forms have been administered} \end{array}$$

$$M_{X_A} = M_{X_B} \quad \text{for each group}$$

$$S_{X_A}^2 = S_{X_B}^2 \quad \text{for each group}$$

That is, two forms of a test (two samples of test items) are considered to be equivalent if they are measuring the same thing, are equally good or bad at doing it, and yield equal means and variances. In short, two forms are equivalent if it doesn't matter which one you give.

Axiom 5: The correlation between error scores on one form of a test and error scores on a parallel form of the same test is equal to zero; i.e., $r_{E_A E_B} = 0$.

This axiom also follows from the concept of random error. If the errors are random, there should be no relationship between the errors on one form of a test and errors on a second form for the same large group of individuals.

Theorem 3: The reliability coefficient of a test is equal to the correlation between the obtained scores on one form of the test and the obtained scores on a parallel form of the same test; that is, $r_{XX} = r_{X_A X_B}$. (Proof given in Appendix, p. 82.)

This theorem is of special importance since it specifies a procedure for actually *calculating* the reliability coefficient of a test. Knowing that the reliability coefficient is equal to the ratio of the true variance to the obtained variance is of theoretical interest but of no practical interest, since we never know the true scores and therefore can not compute their variance. But we *can* administer two parallel forms of a test to a large group of individuals and compute the correlation between scores on form A and scores on form B.

The ultimate objective, however, is to be able to calculate the standard error of measurement so that we can talk about an individual's true and error scores. The formula for the standard error of measurement is given in the following theorem.

Theorem 4: The standard deviation of the errors of measurement, or standard error of measurement, is equal to the standard deviation of the obtained scores times the square root of the quantity 1 minus the reliability coefficient:

$$S_E = S_X \sqrt{1 - r_{X_A X_B}}$$

Proof

By Theorem 2,

$$S_T^2 + S_E^2 = S_X^2$$

But

$$S_T^2 = r_{XX} S_X^2 \quad \text{(by cross-multiplication in Definition 1)}$$

Therefore

$$r_{XX} S_X^2 + S_E^2 = S_X^2$$

Transposing,

$$S_E^2 = S_X^2 - r_{XX} S_X^2$$

Factoring out S_X^2,

$$S_E^2 = S_X^2 (1 - r_{XX})$$

But

$$r_{XX} = r_{X_A X_B} \quad \text{(by Theorem 3)}$$

Therefore

$$S_E^2 = S_X^2 (1 - r_{X_A X_B})$$

Taking the square root of both sides,

$$S_E = S_X \sqrt{1 - r_{X_A X_B}}$$

B. APPLICATIONS

That's enough of the theory. How do we use it?

Let's take the example of the scientific aptitude test referred to on several previous occasions. We administer Form A of the test to half of a large group of individuals and Form B to the other half. A few days later we administer Form B to the half that got Form A the first time and administer Form A to the half that got Form B the first time. (The reason for this "counterbalancing" is to equate across forms any practice effects and/or forgetting effects.) The time between administrations is arbitrary, but should be long enough to provide information as to the stability of the test scores, yet should be short enough so that the students are not exposed to learning experiences that might affect their scores on the second administration.

For each individual we have a Form A score and a Form B score. We calculate the mean and variance for each form and the correlation between the scores on the two forms. Using the formula given in Theorem 4 we calculate the standard error of measurement. For any individual we can draw a picture such as that shown in Figure 4, making the following interpretation of his performance on the test.

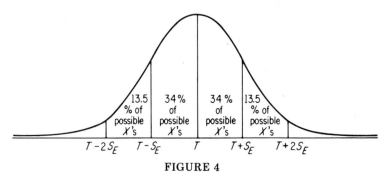

FIGURE 4

Since by Axiom 2 and Axiom 4 error scores are normally distributed with mean zero and standard deviation S_E, 68 percent of an individual's obtained scores fall within one S_E of his true score and 95 percent of his obtained scores fall within two S_E's of his true score. Turning this statement "inside out" we can say that any obtained score for an individual has a 68 percent chance of being within one S_E of his true score, and a 95 percent chance of being within two S_E's of his true score. Saying this still another way: given X, the probability that X is within one S_E of T is .68, and the probability that X is within two S_E's of T is .95.

For a particular illustration let's go back to Johnny, our 13-year-old ninth-grader who got 64 on this scientific aptitude test. Suppose that the authors of the test administered both forms of their test to a representative sample of 500 13-year-old ninth-graders, with the following results:

Form A	Form B
$M = 66.3$	$M = 66.9$
$S^2 = 101.50$	$S^2 = 98.50$

$$r_{X_A X_B} = .84$$

Now according to our theory (Definition 2) the means and variances must be the same, but in actual practice they will not be exactly equal. Since the formula for the standard error of measurement involves the standard deviation of the obtained scores, and since we have two sets of obtained scores, the recommended procedure is to average the variances on the two forms and extract the square root of this "average variance." For the above data we have

$$S_X = \sqrt{\frac{S_{X_A}^2 + S_{X_B}^2}{2}} = \sqrt{\frac{101.50 + 98.50}{2}} = \sqrt{200/2} = \sqrt{100}$$
$$= 10$$

Therefore

$$S_E = 10\sqrt{1 - .84} = 10\sqrt{.16} = 10(.4) = 4$$

Johnny's score of 64 has a 68 percent chance of being within 4 points of his true score and a 95 percent chance of being within 8 points of his true score. "Reasonable limits" for his true score are thus 64 - 8, or 56, and 64 + 8, or 72. These two points define an interval which we are 95 percent sure contains his true score, and is often called in the literature a 95 percent *confidence interval.*

As far as an evaluation of this test with respect to the characteristic of reliability is concerned, if the specification of an

individual's score within a 16-point interval is sufficiently accurate for the purpose for which the test is being used then the
test is acceptable. If not, it's not. Or, relatively speaking, if this
particular test can do a better job than competing tests in yielding close approximations to true scores, it should be chosen for
adoption, all other things being equal. If other tests are more
reliable, this test probably should be discarded unless there are
other compelling reasons, such as lower cost, shorter time, or
better normative data, for keeping it.

There are applications of reliability theory other than the
establishment of confidence intervals for true scores, but they
involve similar reasoning. As an illustration, consider the following problem.

The secondary school that Johnny attends would like to use
this scientific aptitude test for selecting students for an honors
section of biology, and have tentatively set a minimum cut-off
score at a raw score of 85 (maximum possible is 125). Johnny
feels that his performance on the test was far below his true
capabilities, and that he should be selected for this course.
Does he have a case?

In arriving at an answer to this question let us cast the problem within the hypothesis-testing framework treated in Chapter 2. The null hypothesis is that Johnny's true score is at least
as high as 85. The alternative hypothesis is that it is not. The
question is: how likely is it that an individual with a true score
of 85 would get an obtained score of 64? With $S_E = 4$ the
theory tells us that individuals with true scores of 85 on this
test get obtained scores between 81 and 89   68 percent of the
time, and between 77 and 93   95 percent of the time. 2 1/2
percent of the time they will get obtained scores less than 77,
and 2 1/2 percent of the time they will get obtained scores
greater than 93. A score of 64 is less than 77. Therefore the
probability is less than .025 (it's actually less then .00001) that
an individual with a true score of 85 will get an obtained score
of 64 or less.

The most reasonable decision that can be made is to reject
the null hypothesis in favor of the alternative hypothesis—that
is, to tell Johnny that he doesn't have much of a case. This may

be the wrong decision, but the probability of making a wrong decision (type I error) in this instance is less than .00001.

C. OTHER REMARKS CONCERNING RELIABILITY

What do you do if you don't have two forms of a test? As a matter of fact, *not* having two forms of a test is far more common than having them, particularly for teacher-made classroom tests. In this case the recommended procedure is to administer the *same* form twice (so-called *test-retest*), and use the correlation between the scores on the two occasions as an estimate of the reliability coefficient you would have gotten had you had two forms to administer.

What if, for practical or other reasons, you can only administer one form once? Here there are several choices, all unsatisfactory,[1] though some are better than others. The two most common procedures are the *split-half* technique and the *Kuder-Richardson* technique. Both involve the calculation of a coefficient which is, under certain assumptions, an estimate of the parallel-form reliability coefficient.

In the split-half method of estimating test reliability, you divide the test into two halves, traditionally the odd-numbered questions and the even-numbered questions, score each student on each half, calculate the correlation between the half-test scores, and use the following formula, due to Spearman and Brown, for estimating the reliability coefficient of the test:

$$\text{estimated } r_{XX} = \frac{2\, r_{OE}}{1 + r_{OE}} \tag{5-1}$$

where r_{OE} is the correlation between scores on the odd-numbered items and scores on the even-numbered items.

In the Kuder-Richardson method, you need not even do any rescoring or correlating. All that is necessary is to substitute the necessary information into one of the many formulas that were

---

[1] This is my bias showing through. Some authors, for example Cronbach (1970), argue that the best way to estimate the reliability coefficient of a test (he prefers the term *coefficient of generalizability*) is to use Kuder and Richardson's Formula 20 or its more general counterpart, coefficient α. Such authors favor the "internal consistency" approach to reliability rather than the "stability" approach which I personally favor.

derived by Kuder and Richardson by making successive assumptions concerning the test data. The most useful of these, their Formula 20, can be written as

$$\text{estimated } r_{XX} = \frac{k}{k-1} \left[1 - \frac{\Sigma pq}{S_X^2} \right] \qquad (5\text{-}2)$$

where k = number of items on the test, p is the proportion of people answering each item correctly, $q = 1 - p$, and S_X^2 = obtained score variance. In this formula reliability is a function of test length, since the formula involves the number of items on the test. As a matter of fact, the length of a test is always an important factor in the determination of its reliability since, all other things being equal, the longer the test the better it samples the trait being measured and the more likely that an individual's obtained score is close to his true score.

The split-half method for estimating test reliability tends to produce an overestimate of the reliability coefficient, particularly for highly speeded tests. You should be on your guard against authors of tests who report in their test manuals only split-half reliability coefficients. They have perhaps chosen to do so because they have found that their parallel-form or test-retest reliability coefficients are too low!

Finally, in the previous chapter on objectivity I presented several different techniques for determining the degree of objectivity of a test, depending upon the number of students involved and the kind of scale employed. Reliability theory has been developed only for "good," "conceptually continuous" interval scales. For 3-, 4-, and 5-point scales and for essay tests, it is difficult to estimate reliability coefficients and standard errors of measurement.

chapter 6

Validity

A. INTRODUCTION

Authors of standard texts in educational measurement talk about several kinds of validity. There is content validity, construct validity, criterion-related validity, and many other variations of these terms. But for all practical purposes these can be subsumed under two categories—*content validity* and *statistical validity*.

A test is said to have content validity if it appears to be an appropriate measure of some particular trait both because of the way in which the test was developed and because of the makeup of the test items themselves. For example, if our old standby, the scientific aptitude test, was prepared by experienced scientists who started with a definition of scientific aptitude, set down various behaviors that a student must exhibit if he is considered to possess such an aptitude, and constructed test items designed to measure these behaviors, we would say that their test has content validity.

A test is said to have statistical validity if scores on the test are directly related to scores on some generally acceptable external criterion measure of the same or an even more relevant trait. For example, if there is a high positive correlation between scores on the scientific aptitude test and later achievement in science courses, we would say that the test has statistical validity.

Since this book is concerned with the statistical aspects of educational measurement we shall forget about content validity for the time being and concentrate on the property of statistical validity.[1]

[1] I hasten to say, however, that content validity is the more important property since the "generally acceptable external criterion" must have been accepted on the basis of content validity, or on the basis of statistical validity using some other criterion which itself was accepted on the basis of content validity, etc. There must be a measure in the process somewhere which is taken to be *the* criterion.

B. CORRELATION AND PREDICTION

The investigation of the statistical validity of a test involves the correlation of scores on the test with scores on some external criterion, be that another already widely accepted test, teachers' grades, or what-have-you. If the correlation between the test and the criterion is high, the test is valid. If the correlation is low, it isn't. But how high is high and how low is low? Much depends upon the magnitude of the correlation relative to the magnitude of the correlations between other competing tests and this criterion or comparable criteria. It just so happens that for many traits, particularly those in the personality, or "affective," domain, correlations between tests and criteria rarely exceed .40, whereas for many "cognitive" areas (reading is one) correlations of .60 and .70 are quite common.

The coefficient of correlation between a test and a criterion is called, naturally enough, a *validity coefficient*. In the discussion that follows it will be assumed that the correlation coefficients are Pearson product-moment correlation coefficients, but there are applications of correlations between test and criterion where the rank-correlation coefficient, the index of order association (both treated in Chapter 4), or some other coefficient, is the appropriate statistic to use.[2]

Closely related to the matter of correlation is that of prediction, as pointed out in Chapter 3. If the correlation between a test and a criterion is high, predictions of criterion performance are quite accurate. If this correlation is low, predictions are poor.

In addition to the validity coefficient, then, another indication of the validity of a test is the accuracy with which one can predict an individual's criterion score from a knowledge of his test score. The statistic which is used as a measure of the accuracy of prediction is the *standard error of estimate*, or the *standard error of prediction*, which I shall define and for which I shall derive a formula below. This statistic is analogous to the standard error of measurement treated in the previous chapter on test reliability, as the validity coefficient is analogous to the reliability coefficient.

[2] Another very popular way of treating statistical validity is through the use of *expectancy tables*. See for example Cronbach (1970).

You may recall that in the derivation of the Pearson product-moment correlation coefficient the starting point was the equation $z_Y = mz_X$, or actually $z'_Y = mz_X$, which was the equation of the straight line which best fit the points. This equation, which I will write in the form $z'_Y = r_{XY}z_X$, since $m = r_{XY}$, is also the equation for *predicting* standard score on Y from standard score on X. In the investigation of the statistical validity of a test, X denotes raw score on the test and Y denotes raw score on the criterion. Knowing r_{XY} and knowing an individual's z_X, we can use this prediction equation to calculate z'_Y, his predicted standard score on Y. The question is: how sure are we of our prediction? The answer is arrived at as follows.

For the sample of individuals upon whom our determination of r_{XY} was based, all individuals having the same z_X did not have the same z_Y (unless the correlation was perfect), but for these individuals the z_Y's "averaged out" to a value of z'_Y, determined by the equation $z'_Y = r_{XY}z_X$, since this was the equation of the line of best fit to the points. If we assume that the particular individual whose criterion performance we are trying to predict, and other individuals for whom predictions could be made, will "behave" just as those in the original sample did, we expect that individuals in this group with the same z_X will get various z_Y's as did those in the original sample, and that the average of *their* z_Y's will also be the z'_Y calculated by $z'_Y = r_{XY}z_X$. We will thus predict the same criterion performance for all individuals who have the same test performance and will use some measure of the spread of the actual z_Y's around the predicted z_Y, for the original sample, as an indication of the accuracy of prediction.

The most common measure of spread is the variance (or standard deviation). We determine the variance of the z_Y's around z'_Y as follows.

By definition,

$$\text{Variance} = \frac{\Sigma (z_Y - z'_Y)^2}{N}$$

$$= \frac{1}{N} \Sigma (z_Y - r_{XY}z_X)^2 \qquad (\text{since } z'_Y = r_{XY}z_X)$$

$$= \frac{1}{N} \Sigma (z_Y^2 - 2r_{XY}z_Xz_Y + r_{XY}^2z_X^2) \qquad (\text{by expansion})$$

$$= \frac{1}{N} \left[\Sigma z_Y^2 - 2r_{XY} \Sigma z_X z_Y + r_{XY}^2 \Sigma z_X^2 \right] \qquad \text{(by Formulas A-1 and A-2 of Appendix)}$$

$$= \frac{\Sigma z_Y^2}{N} - 2r_{XY} \frac{\Sigma z_X z_Y}{N} + r_{XY}^2 \frac{\Sigma z_X^2}{N} \qquad \text{(multiplying through by } 1/N)$$

$$= \frac{N}{N} - 2r_{XY} (r_{XY}) + r_{XY}^2 \cdot \frac{N}{N}$$

$$= 1 - 2r_{XY}^2 + r_{XY}^2$$

$$= 1 - r_{XY}^2 \qquad \text{(since by Formula A-4 of Appendix}$$

$$\Sigma z_Y^2 = \Sigma z_X^2 = N, \text{ and since } \frac{\Sigma z_X z_Y}{N} = r_{XY})$$

Whenever z_Y is not equal to z_Y' we have made an error in prediction. $z_Y - z_Y'$ is a measure of the error of prediction, and the variance just determined is thus the variance of the errors of prediction. The square root of this quantity is the standard deviation of the errors of prediction, abbreviated to the standard error of prediction, or more commonly referred to as the *standard error of estimate* (since predicting and estimating are essentially the same thing). The notation for this statistic is $S_{z_Y \cdot z_X}$, the S indicating standard deviation and the $z_Y \cdot z_X$ subscript indicating that z_Y is being predicted[3] from z_X. Thus

$$S_{z_Y \cdot z_X} = \sqrt{1 - r_{XY}^2} \qquad (6\text{-}1)$$

How do we use the standard error of prediction? The following is an illustration.

Let's go back to Johnny, who got a raw score of 64 on the scientific aptitude test. Since the mean score for this test for the normative sample was 66.6 (the average of M_{X_A} and M_{X_B})

[3] If you are interested in predicting Y rather than z_Y, from X, rather than from z_X, the prediction equation becomes

$$Y' = r_{XY} \frac{S_Y}{S_X} X + \left(M_Y - r_{XY} \frac{S_Y}{S_X} M_X \right)$$

and the formula for the standard error of predicting Y from X is

$$S_Y \cdot X = S_Y \sqrt{1 - r_{XY}^2}$$

and the standard deviation is 10, his $z_X = \dfrac{64 - 66.6}{10} = \dfrac{-2.6}{10} =$
$-.26$, or about a quarter of a standard deviation below the mean.

Suppose that the correlation between scores on this test and scores on a standardized achievement test in biology is .60. Using the prediction equation, we predict that Johnny's standard score on the achievement test would be .60 $(-.26) = -.16$, or about 1/6th of a standard deviation below the mean criterion score.

But the standard deviation of the errors of prediction = $\sqrt{1 - r_{XY}^2} = \sqrt{1 - (.60)^2} = \sqrt{1 - .36} = \sqrt{.64} = .80$. Assuming that these errors are normally distributed, 68 percent of all individuals who get a z_X of $-.26$ will get z_Y's between $-.16 - .80$ and $-.16 + .80$—i.e., between $-.96$ and .64. 95 percent of all individuals who get a z_X of $-.26$ will get z_Y's between $-.16 - 2(.80)$ and $-.16 + 2(.80)$—i.e., between -1.76 and 1.44.

Therefore since Johnny is one of the individuals who got a z_X of $-.26$ we are "95 percent sure" that his z_Y will be between -1.76 and 1.44, and these are therefore "reasonable limits" for his criterion performance. If this interval, which is another kind of confidence interval, is acceptable for the purpose for which we are making the prediction, this test is statistically valid. If not, it's not. Or again, as was true for test reliability, if this test does a better job than competing tests as far as prediction is concerned, it should be retained. If not, the dropping of such a test and the adoption of another should be considered.

You may feel that an interval of -1.76 to 1.44 has not "narrowed things down" very much, since the entire standard score range is typically from -2.5 to 2.5. Well, you are right. For validity coefficients below about .70, prediction is a very discouraging endeavor. The governing factor is the r_{XY}^2 in the formula for the standard error of prediction. For r_{XY}'s less than $\sqrt{.5}$, r_{XY}^2 is less than .5, which means that $S_{z_Y \cdot z_X}$ is greater than .5, or greater than one-half of the standard deviation of the z_Y scores themselves. For test *reliability* the governing factor in the width of the confidence interval for an individual's true score is the $r_{X_A X_B}$ (the reliability coefficient) in the formula for the standard error of measurement, which is *not* squared. Furthermore, reliability coefficients run higher than validity coefficients, so that $1 - r_{X_A X_B}$ is *much* smaller than $1 - r_{XY}^2$. The only consolation is that it makes sense that we are better able to estimate an individual's true score on a test than to estimate his score on another variable from his score on the given test; i.e., that a test is a better measure of itself than it is of something else.

C. ATTENUATION

At the beginning of Chapter 4 I made the statement that a test can not be valid unless it is reliable, since if we have scores on two forms of a test for the same group of individuals, and if these scores are quite different from one another, we do not know which set to use to compare with a set of criterion scores. Actually it is a matter of degree; a test with a high reliability coefficient is more likely to have a high validity coefficient than a test with a low reliability coefficient. Unreliability in both the test and the criterion results in lower correlation between test and criterion.

It is of theoretical interest to have a way of estimating what the correlation between test and criterion would be if neither were subject to measurement error. In other words, we would like to know what the correlation between *true scores* on the test and *true scores* on the criterion would be. The traditional formula for estimating the correlation between true scores on X and true scores on Y, as derived in the Appendix, p. 83, is:

$$r_{T_X T_Y} = \frac{r_{XY}}{\sqrt{r_{XX}} \sqrt{r_{YY}}} \qquad (6\text{-}2)$$

where r_{XX} and r_{YY} are the reliability coefficients for X and Y, respectively.

For example, if test X, which has reliability coefficient .64, correlates .36 with criterion Y, which has reliability coefficient .81, the correlation between true scores on X and true scores on Y is $\dfrac{.36}{\sqrt{.64}\sqrt{.81}} = \dfrac{.36}{.80\,(.90)} = \dfrac{.36}{.72} = .50$.

This formula for estimating the correlation between true scores on X and true scores on Y is often called the *correction for attenuation* formula for the validity coefficient, since the answer is itself a validity coefficient not subject to measurement error, unreliability, or restriction due to test length. Obtained test scores X and obtained criterion scores Y *are* subject to this restriction (this attenuation), and should be "corrected" therefor.

We can also use the same formula to determine the maximum possible correlation between any two variables X and Y. The maximum possible correlation will be obtained when there is perfect relationship between true scores on the two variables, i.e., when $r_{T_X T_Y} = 1$. Substituting this in Eq. 6-2 and solving for r_{XY} we have:

$$\text{maximum possible } r_{XY} = \sqrt{r_{XX}}\ \sqrt{r_{YY}} \qquad (6\text{-}3)$$

In words, the maximum possible correlation between any two variables X and Y is the product of the square roots of their reliability coefficients. In the example just given, if $r_{XX} = .64$ and $r_{YY} = .81$ the largest validity coefficient that one could ever get for two such measures is $\sqrt{.64} \cdot \sqrt{.81} = .80\ (.90) = .72$, even if there is perfect correlation between true scores on the two variables.

Thus the reliability of a test plays a crucial role in determining validity coefficients for that test. Even when the criterion is perfectly reliable, the validity coefficient is restricted by the test's reliability coefficient, since in that case the maximum possible $r_{XY} = \sqrt{r_{XX}}\ \sqrt{1} = \sqrt{r_{XX}}$. For the test in the example under consideration, its maximum possible obtained validity coefficient with a perfectly reliable criterion is equal to $\sqrt{.64} = .80$.

chapter 7

Item Analysis

Up to this point we have been concerned with tests as single entities. Only in conjunction with the split-half and Kuder-Richardson techniques for estimating test reliability did we even mention the possibility of analyzing the test in parts rather than as a whole. In this chapter we shall consider some of the traditional methods for breaking up a test into its component items and investigating various characteristics of the items themselves.

One thing we always like to know about an item is its *difficulty*. As is so aptly pointed out in measurement textbooks, an item which is answered correctly by all examinees is an unacceptable item from the point of view of relative measurement, since the only effect it has is to add one point to everybody's score. An item which is answered *incorrectly* by all examinees is similarly unacceptable.

The way we determine the difficulty of an item, of course, is to calculate the percentage of individuals who answer the item correctly. If this percentage is high, the item is said to be "easy"; if the percentage is low, the item is said to be "hard." For example, if 39 percent of a group of individuals answer a given test item correctly the item is said to have an item difficulty of 39 percent, or .39, and is thus a fairly hard item.

Closely related to item difficulty is the matter of item *discrimination* or how well the item serves to distinguish between those who know the material and those who do not. There are many ways of determining the discriminating power of a test item, but they fall into two distinct categories:

1. Those procedures which use total score on the test itself to identify "those who know the material" and "those who do not."
2. Those procedures which use scores on some external criterion for this purpose.

The first of these methods is by far the more common, and the item-test comparisons yield *internal consistency* measures for the items. The second method, though less commonly employed, is far better since the item-criterion comparisons yield actual *validity coefficients* for the *items.*

Regardless of the method adopted—whether it be for the purpose of obtaining item-test or item-criterion discrimination indices—the first step is the identification of the "know" and "don't know" groups. For item-test comparisons this typically involves the ordering of individuals by total test score and selecting some percentage of these as the "knows," or "high" group, and some percentage of these as the "don't knows," or "low" group. The traditional procedure is to choose the top 27 percent for the high group and the bottom 27 percent for the low group. The figure 27 percent is arbitrary, but it has been shown, by the late Truman Kelley and others, that this percentage has important statistical properties, and for most applications 27 percent is small enough to identify clearly high and clearly low performers, yet large enough to provide a sufficient number of scores as a basis for the item statistics.

Having identified the extreme groups we determine for each group the percentage of individuals who answer correctly each of the items on the test. The difference between the percentage of individuals in the high group who answer the item correctly and the percentage of individuals in the low group who answer the item correctly, or some function of this difference, is taken as the measure of item discrimination. Extensive tables such as those of Fan (1952) have been prepared whereby one enters the table with the high-group percentage and the low-group percentage and reads directly the value of the *biserial correlation coefficient* between item performance and total test score, under the assumption that the test scores are normally distributed and that the item scores have an underlying trait distribution which is also normal.

For item-criterion comparisons the procedure is the same except that the "high" and "low" groups are determined by total criterion score rather than total test score. Again, these groups are traditionally taken to be the top 27 percent and the bottom 27 percent.

As an example of each of these procedures, suppose that a

given test item on our scientific aptitude test were answered correctly by 80 percent of the high group (by total test score) and by 40 percent of the low group on this test. This item would be a *positively discriminating* item as far as internal consistency of the test is concerned; whatever the test is measuring this particular item is measuring essentially the same thing. If this same item were answered correctly by 50 percent of a group with high total scores on a subsequently administered scientific achievement test and by 60 percent of a low-scoring group, the item would be a *negatively discriminating* item, as far as validity is concerned, in that those who had low achievement (criterion) scores performed better on the item than those who had high achievement scores.

Measures of item difficulty and item discrimination are very useful as far as test revision is concerned. All other things being equal, we should retain items that are of medium difficulty and are positively discriminating, discarding or "patching up" those that are either too hard or too easy and those which fail to discriminate or do so in the negative direction.

chapter 8

Sampling and Tests
of Significance

SAMPLING

In the development of a test, in the compilation of norms for a standardized test, and in carrying out studies of test reliability and validity, we are constantly faced with sampling problems. Each item on a test should be representative of the set of all possible items that we *could* put in the test. The norm group which serves as the basis for the interpretation of the scores obtained by individuals who subsequently take the test should constitute a large, representative sample of the population in which we are interested. Statistical validity coefficients should be based on large, representative samples of the kinds of students for whom we would like to make predictions.

The two most desirable sampling procedures are *simple random sampling* and *stratified random sampling.* In selecting a simple random sample we must first make a list of all of the objects in the population of interest (items, people, schools) and then choose a subset of objects in such a way that each subset has an equal chance of being drawn. The best way to assure this is to assign a serial number to each object and to utilize a table of random numbers for drawing the sample. Most standard statistics textbooks, such as Tate (1965), contain one or more of such tables and provide directions for their use.

An easier procedure for approximately a simple random sample once the entire population has been enumerated is to determine the population-to-sample ratio (e.g. 10 to 1) and to select every nth object (say every tenth object), beginning with an arbitrarily chosen starting point. This gives every object an essentially equal chance of being drawn and is sufficiently random for all practical purposes.

A stratified random sample differs from a simple random sample in only one major respect. Prior to the selection of the sample the population is divided into various subpopulations, or strata, and a simple random sample is drawn *from each stratum.* The principal advantage of doing this is that the composite sample actually selected is certain to contain representatives of each stratum. For example, if a population of fifth-graders is first stratified by sex and simple random samples of boys and of girls are drawn, the sample must contain pupils of both sexes. A simple random sample of a population of fifth-graders may contain no girls at all, or no boys, even if the population has an equal number of girls and boys, particularly if the size of the sample is small.

There are two principal disadvantages of stratified random sampling. The first is that the technique can become quite complicated if the population is stratified on more than one variable at a time (e.g., sex and age). A second disadvantage is that most of the procedures for carrying out tests of statistical significance, to which I would now like to turn, assume simple random rather than stratified random sampling.

TESTS OF SIGNIFICANCE

"The difference between the means is significant at the .05 level." "The relationship between the variables is significant at the .01 level."

Statements like these are frequently encountered in professional journals which contain descriptions of educational and psychological research studies. But they are also found in manuals and/or technical reports for standardized tests. What do they mean?

Tests of significance are statistical inferential procedures for determining the extent to which a result which has been obtained in a sample is likely to have occurred by chance. Results which resemble chance findings are of no particular interest. Results which are unlikely to have occurred by chance are usually interpreted as "real," or substantive, findings.

There are three very common tests of significance that the student of educational measurement is likely to come across in his study of standardized tests. One is the "*t*" test of the significance of the difference between two independent sample means. The second is the "*t*" test of the significance of a Pearson product-moment correlation coefficient. The third is the chi-square (χ^2) test of the significance of the relationship between two nominal (categorical) or ordinal variables. Only a brief explanation of these procedures will be considered here. The interested reader can pursue the finer points of these and other more advanced statistical inferential tests in any good text in statistical methods, e.g., Hays (1963).

Since these procedures are most likely to be encountered in investigating the statistical validity of a test, I shall treat them all in that context.

1. Suppose our favorite scientific aptitude test was given to a representative sample of 52 ninth-graders in the fall of the school year. During the tenth grade they all took a course in biology. Half of them obtained grades of C or better; the other half obtained grades of D or E. The means and standard deviations on the aptitude test for these two groups, and the number of pupils in each group, were as follows:

Group 1 (C or better)	Group 2 (D or E)
$M = 85$	$M = 60$
$S = 20$	$S = 25$
$N = 26$	$N = 26$

The question related to the validity of the aptitude test is: Was there a statistically significant difference between the mean aptitude scores of those who did well in biology (grade of C or better) and those who did not do well (grade of D or E)? If the difference is significant (in favor of those who did well) then we have some evidence that the aptitude test is valid—i.e., those who get high scores on the test tend to get good biology grades. If the difference is not significant, the test is of dubious validity.

This problem can be treated in the hypothesis-testing framework first introduced in Chapter 2. The null hypothesis is that there is no difference in mean aptitude score between good and poor biology students. The alternative hypothesis is that good biology students have higher mean aptitude scores than poor biology students. The decision to accept or reject the null hypothesis is based on probabilities associated with the t-distribution (rather than on binomial probabilities as in Chapter 2 or normal probabilities as in Chapter 5). The formula for t and the rationale for arriving at a decision with respect to this null hypothesis are as follows, the subscripts referring to the groups:

$$t = \frac{M_1 - M_2}{\sqrt{\dfrac{N_1 + N_2}{N_1 N_2} \cdot \dfrac{N_1 S_1^2 + N_2 S_2^2}{N_1 + N_2 - 2}}} \tag{8-1}$$

$$= \frac{85 - 60}{\sqrt{\dfrac{26 + 26}{26\,(26)} \cdot \dfrac{26\,(400) + 26\,(625)}{26 + 26 - 2}}}$$

$$= \frac{25}{\sqrt{\dfrac{52}{676} \cdot \dfrac{26650}{50}}}$$

$$= \frac{25}{\sqrt{41}}$$

$$= \frac{25}{6.40}$$

$$= 3.91$$

Referring this value to the appropriate statistical table we find that a difference of 25 points is likely to occur by chance less than one time in one thousand, i.e., $P < .001$. Our best decision is to reject the null hypothesis and conclude that good students did have significantly higher aptitude scores. The aptitude test therefore possesses substantial predictive validity for these students.

2. Suppose that we also had scores on a standardized achievement test in biology taken by these same students at the end of the tenth grade and that the correlation (Pearson product-moment r) between their aptitude scores and their achievement scores was equal to .60. Is this a "significant" relationship?

The procedure for answering this question is very similar to the procedure just described. The only major modifications are that we have different null and alternative hypotheses and a different "t" formula. They are:

Null hypothesis: There is no relationship between aptitude and achievement scores.

Alternative hypothesis: There is a relationship between aptitude and achievement scores.

$$t = \frac{r}{\sqrt{\dfrac{1 - r^2}{N - 2}}} \tag{8-2}$$

where N is the total sample size, from which

$$t = \frac{.60}{\sqrt{\dfrac{1 - (.60)^2}{52 - 2}}}$$

$$= \frac{.60}{\sqrt{.0128}}$$

$$= \frac{.60}{.18}$$

$$= 5.45$$

Looking up this value in the table of the t-distribution we find that a correlation coefficient of .60 is also less than .1 percent likely to have occurred by chance—i.e., $P < .001$. The corresponding null hypothesis should be rejected, and we have further evidence of the predictive validity of the aptitude test.

3. Finally, suppose that at the end of the tenth grade each student indicated on a three-point scale (yes, no, undecided) whether he (she) wanted to take chemistry in the eleventh grade. The results, cross-tabulated with their performance on the aptitude test, were as follows:

		Yes	No	Undecided	Totals
	Above the mean	(12) 15	(7) 4	(8) 7	26
Aptitude score	Below the mean	(12) 9	(7) 10	(8) 9	26
	Totals	24	14	16	52

Is there a significant relationship between aptitude score and preference for studying chemistry?

Null hypothesis: There is no relationship between aptitude and preference.

Test statistic: $\chi^2 = \dfrac{(f_o - f_e)^2}{f_e}$ (8-3)

where the summation is over all six cells of the above table and where f_o = observed frequency in each cell, and f_e = expected frequency (in parentheses) if there were absolutely no relationship between the two variables.

$$\chi^2 = \frac{(15 - 12)^2}{12} + \frac{(4 - 7)^2}{7} + \frac{(7 - 8)^2}{8} + \frac{(9 - 12)^2}{12}$$
$$+ \frac{(10 - 7)^2}{7} + \frac{(9 - 8)^2}{8}$$

$$= \frac{9}{12} + \frac{9}{7} + \frac{1}{8} + \frac{9}{12} + \frac{9}{7} + \frac{1}{8}$$

$$= \frac{726}{168}$$

$$= 4.32$$

Referring this value to a table of the χ^2 distribution we find that discrepancies between the actual observed frequencies and the expected frequencies could occur by chance more than ten times in one hundred. We therefore do not reject the null hypothesis. The test has little validity regarding preference for studying chemistry even though it has substantial validity for predicting biology grades and for predicting performance on a standardized biology achievement test.

Appendix

I. RULES FOR OPERATING WITH SUMMATION SIGNS

Many of the derivations and proofs contained in the text and in this appendix make use of the following formulas. (In each case the summation is over the number of individuals N.)

$$\Sigma \, cf(X) = c\Sigma f(X) \tag{A-1}$$

$$\Sigma \, [f_1 \, (X) + f_2 \, (X) + \cdots] = \Sigma f_1 \, (X) + \Sigma f_2 \, (X) + \cdots \tag{A-2}$$

$$\Sigma c = Nc \tag{A-3}$$

Formula A-1 states that summing a constant times a function of the variable X is the same as summing the function and then multiplying by the constant. For example, $\Sigma \, 3X^2 = 3\Sigma X^2$. What this formula says, in effect, is that the constant can be "factored out" or "brought outside the summation sign" since it is common to all individuals.

Formula A-2 states that summing a function which is itself a sum of functions and summing the component functions lead to the same result. For example, $\Sigma \, (X + X^2) = \Sigma X + \Sigma X^2$. What this formula indicates is that since you are "adding everything in sight" it doesn't really matter how you group the terms, so that the summation sign can be "distributed" to the various components.

Formula A-3 states that if you add a constant to itself N times you get an answer which is equal to N times the constant. This is actually a definition of the operation of multiplication.

II. DERIVATION OF RELATIONSHIPS BETWEEN STANDARD DEVIATION AND RANGE, FORMULAS 3-4 AND 3-5

Let X_H be the highest score obtained by any individual in a group of N individuals, and let X_L be the lowest score. Then the range, R, $= X_H - X_L$.

The standard deviation will be *minimum* if all of the other scores are located right at the mean and if the mean is located halfway between X_H and X_L, i.e., if $M = \dfrac{X_H + X_L}{2}$. In this case the only nonzero deviations from the mean will be those for X_H and X_L, and the variance, $S^2_{\min}$, will be determined as follows:

$$S^2_{\min} = \frac{\Sigma (X - M)^2}{N}$$

$$= \frac{1}{N} \left[(X_H - M)^2 + (X_L - M)^2 \right]$$

$$= \frac{1}{N} \left[\left(X_H - \frac{X_H + X_L}{2} \right)^2 + \left(X_L - \frac{X_H + X_L}{2} \right)^2 \right]$$

$$= \frac{1}{N} \left[\left(X_H - \frac{X_H}{2} - \frac{X_L}{2} \right)^2 + \left(X_L - \frac{X_H}{2} - \frac{X_L}{2} \right)^2 \right]$$

$$= \frac{1}{N} \left(\frac{X_H - X_L}{2} \right)^2 + \left(- \frac{X_H - X_L}{2} \right)^2 \right]$$

$$= \frac{1}{N} \left[(R/2)^2 + (-R/2)^2 \right]$$

$$= \frac{1}{N} (R^2/4 + R^2/4)$$

$$= \frac{1}{N} (R^2/2)$$

$$= \frac{R^2}{2N}$$

Therefore,

$$S_{\min} = \sqrt{\frac{R^2}{2N}} = \frac{R}{\sqrt{2N}} = \frac{\text{range}}{\sqrt{2N}}$$

The standard deviation will be *maximum* if half of the individuals get a score of X_H and the other half of the individuals get a score of X_L. In this case $M = \dfrac{X_H + X_L}{2}$ also, and all of the deviations from the mean are either $R/2$ or $-R/2$. Thus,

$$S^2_{\max} = \frac{\Sigma (X - M)^2}{N}$$

$$= \frac{1}{N} [N/2 \, (R/2)^2 + N/2 \, (-R/2)^2]$$

$$= \frac{1}{N} (NR^2/8 + NR^2/8)$$

$$= \frac{1}{N} (NR^2/4)$$

$$= \frac{R^2}{4}$$

Therefore,

$$S_{\max} = \sqrt{R^2/4} = R/2 = \frac{\text{range}}{2}$$

III. PROOF THAT STANDARD SCORES HAVE MEAN 0 AND VARIANCE 1

$$M_z = \frac{\Sigma z}{N}$$

$$= \frac{1}{N} \sum \left(\frac{X - M}{S}\right) \quad \text{(by 3-6)}$$

$$= \frac{1}{NS} \Sigma (X - M) \quad \text{(by A-1)}$$

$$= \frac{1}{NS} (\Sigma X - \Sigma M) \quad \text{(by A-2)}$$

$$= \frac{1}{NS} (\Sigma X - NM) \quad \text{(by A-3)}$$

$$= \frac{1}{NS} (NM - NM) \quad \left(\text{since } M = \frac{\Sigma X}{N}, \ \Sigma X = NM\right)$$

$$= 0$$

$$S^2_z = \frac{\Sigma (z - M_z)^2}{N}$$

$$= \frac{\Sigma z^2}{N} \quad \text{(since, from above, } M_z = 0)$$

$$= \frac{1}{N} \sum \left(\frac{X - M}{S} \right)^2 \quad \text{(by 3-7)}$$

$$= \frac{1}{NS^2} \Sigma (X - M)^2 \quad \text{(by A-1)}$$

$$= \frac{1}{NS^2} (NS^2) \quad \left(\text{since if } S^2 = \frac{\Sigma (X - M)^2}{N}, \right.$$
$$\left. \Sigma (X - M)^2 = NS^2 \right)$$

$$= 1$$

(Also, $S_z = \sqrt{S_z^2} = \sqrt{1} = 1$.)

Since $\frac{\Sigma_z^2}{N} = 1$, we have:

$$\Sigma_Z{}^2 = N \qquad (A\text{-}4)$$

IV. PROOF OF THEOREM 2

$$S_X^2 = \frac{\Sigma (X - M_X)^2}{N}$$

$$= \frac{1}{N} \left[\Sigma (X^2 - 2M_X X + M_X^2) \right] \quad \text{(by expansion)}$$

$$= \frac{1}{N} (\Sigma X^2 - 2M_X \Sigma X + NM_X^2) \quad \text{(by A-1, A-2, and A-3)}$$

$$= \frac{1}{N} \left[\Sigma X^2 - 2M_X (NM_X) + NM_X^2 \right] \quad \text{(since } \Sigma X = NM_X)$$

$$= \frac{1}{N} (\Sigma X^2 - NM_X^2) \qquad (A\text{-}5)$$

$$= \frac{1}{N} \left[\Sigma (T + E)^2 - NM_T^2 \right] \quad \text{(by Axiom 1 and Theorem 1)}$$

$$= \frac{1}{N} \left[\Sigma (T^2 + 2TE + E^2) - NM_T^2 \right] \quad \text{(by expansion)}$$

$$= \frac{1}{N} (\Sigma T^2 + 2\Sigma TE + \Sigma E^2 - NM_T^2) \quad \text{(by A-1 and A-2)}$$

$$= \frac{1}{N} (\Sigma T^2 - NM_T^2 + \Sigma E^2 + 2\Sigma TE) \quad \text{(by rearranging)}$$

$$= \frac{1}{N} (\Sigma T^2 - NM_T^2 + \Sigma E^2 - NM_E^2 + 2\Sigma TE) \qquad \text{(since } M_E = 0)$$

$$= \frac{1}{N} (\Sigma T^2 - NM_T^2) + \frac{1}{N} (\Sigma E^2 - NM_E^2) + \frac{1}{N} (2\Sigma TE)$$

$$= S_T^2 + S_E^2 + \frac{2\Sigma TE}{N} \qquad \text{(by A-5)}$$

$$r_{XY} = \frac{\Sigma z_X z_Y}{N} = \frac{\Sigma (X - M_X)(Y - M_Y)}{NS_X S_Y} \qquad \text{(by 3-7, 3-6, and A-1)}$$

$$= \frac{\Sigma XY - M_X \Sigma Y - M_Y \Sigma X + \Sigma M_X M_Y}{NS_X S_Y} \qquad \text{(by A-1 and A-2)}$$

$$= \frac{\Sigma XY - M_X (NM_Y) - M_Y (NM_X) + NM_X M_Y}{NS_X S_Y}$$
$$\text{(since } \Sigma X = NM_X \text{ and } \Sigma Y = NM_Y \text{, and by A-3)}$$

$$= \frac{\Sigma XY - NM_X M_Y}{NS_X S_Y} \tag{A-6}$$

If $X = T$ and $Y = E$, then

$$r_{TE} = \frac{\Sigma TE - NM_T M_E}{NS_T S_E}$$

But by Axiom 3,

$$r_{TE} = 0$$

Therefore,

$$\Sigma TE - NM_T M_E = 0 \qquad \text{(since if a fraction equals 0 its}$$
$$\text{numerator must equal 0)}$$

Therefore,

$$\Sigma TE = 0 \qquad \text{(since } M_E = 0 \text{ by Axiom 2)}$$

Therefore,

$$\frac{2\Sigma TE}{N} = 0$$

Therefore,

$$S_X^2 = S_T^2 + S_E^2$$

V. PROOF OF THEOREM 3

$$r_{X_AX_B} = \frac{\Sigma X_AX_B - NM_{X_A}M_{X_B}}{NS_{X_A}S_{X_B}} \quad \text{(by A-6)}$$

$$= \frac{\Sigma X_AX_B - NM_X^2}{NS_X^2} \quad \text{(since } M_{X_A} = M_{X_B} = M_X \text{ and } S_{X_A} = S_{X_B} = S_X \text{ by Definition 2)}$$

$$= \frac{1}{NS_X^2}[\Sigma(T + E_A)(T + E_B) - NM_T^2] \quad \text{(by Axiom 1 and Theorem 1)}$$

$$= \frac{1}{NS_X^2}[\Sigma(T^2 + TE_A + TE_B + E_AE_B) - NM_T^2] \quad \text{(by expansion)}$$

$$= \frac{1}{NS_X^2}[(\Sigma T^2 + \Sigma TE_A + \Sigma TE_B + \Sigma E_AE_B) - NM_T^2] \quad \text{(by A-2)}$$

$$= \frac{1}{NS_X^2}(\Sigma T^2 - NM_T^2) + \frac{1}{NS_X^2}(\Sigma TE_A + \Sigma TE_B + \Sigma E_AE_B) \quad \text{(by rearranging)}$$

$$= \frac{S_T^2}{S_X^2} + \frac{1}{NS_X^2}(\Sigma TE_A + \Sigma TE_B + \Sigma E_AE_B) \quad \text{(by A-5)}$$

But

$$r_{TE_A} = \frac{\Sigma TE_A - NM_TM_{E_A}}{NS_TS_{E_A}} = 0 \quad \text{(by A-6 and Axiom 3)}$$

Therefore,

$$\Sigma TE_A - NM_TM_{E_A} = 0$$

Therefore,

$$\Sigma TE_A = 0$$

Similarly,

$$\Sigma TE_B = 0$$

Also,

$$r_{E_AE_B} = \frac{\Sigma E_AE_B - NM_{E_A}M_{E_B}}{NS_{E_A}S_{E_B}} = 0 \quad \text{(by A-6 and Axiom 5)}$$

Therefore,

$$\Sigma E_A E_B - N M_{E_A} M_{E_B} = 0$$

Therefore,

$$\Sigma E_A E_B = 0$$

Therefore,

$$r_{X_A X_B} = \frac{S_T^2}{S_X^2} = r_{XX} \qquad \text{(by Definition 1)}$$

VI. DERIVATION OF THE FORMULA FOR THE CORRELATION BETWEEN TRUE SCORES ON TEST X AND TRUE SCORES ON CRITERION Y, FORMULA 6-2

$$r_{T_X T_Y} = \frac{\Sigma T_X T_Y - N M_{T_X} M_{T_Y}}{N S_{T_X} S_{T_Y}} \qquad \text{(by A-6)}$$

$$= \frac{\Sigma (X - E_X)(Y - E_Y) - N M_X M_Y}{N \sqrt{r_{XX} S_X^2} \sqrt{r_{YY} S_Y^2}}$$

(by Axiom 1, Theorem 1, and Definition 1)

$$= \frac{\Sigma (XY - E_Y X + E_X E_Y) - N M_X M_Y}{N S_X S_Y \sqrt{r_{XX}} \sqrt{r_{YY}}}$$

(by expanding and simplifying)

$$= \frac{\Sigma XY - \Sigma E_X Y - \Sigma E_Y X + \Sigma E_X E_Y - N M_X M_Y}{N S_X S_Y \sqrt{r_{XX}} \sqrt{r_{YY}}}$$

(by A-2)

$$= \frac{\Sigma XY - N M_X M_Y}{N S_X S_Y \sqrt{r_{XX}} \sqrt{r_{YY}}} - \frac{\Sigma E_X Y + \Sigma E_Y X - \Sigma E_X E_Y}{N S_X S_Y \sqrt{r_{XX}} \sqrt{r_{YY}}}$$

(by rearranging)

If error scores are truly random, the correlation between error scores on X and obtained scores on Y, the correlation between error scores on Y and obtained scores on X, and the correlation between error scores on X and error scores on Y will all be equal to zero:

$$r_{E_X Y} = r_{E_Y X} = r_{E_X E_Y} = 0$$

But

$$r_{E_X Y} = \frac{\Sigma E_X Y - N M_{E_X} M_Y}{N S_{E_X} S_Y} \quad \text{(by A-6)}$$

Therefore,

$$\Sigma E_X Y - N M_{E_X} M_Y = 0$$

Therefore,

$$\Sigma E_X Y = 0 \quad \text{(since } M_{E_X} = 0 \text{ by Axiom 2)}$$

Similarly,

$$\Sigma E_Y X = 0 \quad \text{and} \quad \Sigma E_X E_Y = 0$$

Therefore,

$$r_{T_X T_Y} = \frac{\Sigma XY - N M_X M_Y}{N S_X S_Y \sqrt{r_{XX}} \sqrt{r_{YY}}}$$

But

$$\frac{\Sigma XY - N M_X M_Y}{N S_X S_Y} = r_{XY} \quad \text{(by A-6)}$$

Therefore,

$$r_{T_X T_Y} = \frac{r_{XY}}{\sqrt{r_{XX}} \sqrt{r_{YY}}}$$

References

Cronbach, Lee J. *Essentials of Psychological Testing.* 3d ed. New York: Harper, 1970.

Ebel, Robert L. *Measuring Educational Achievement.* Englewood Cliffs, N.J.: Prentice-Hall, 1965.

Fan, Chung-teh. *Item Analysis Table.* Princeton, N.J.: Educational Testing Service, 1952.

Furst, Edward J. *Constructing Evaluation Instruments.* New York: Longmans, 1958.

Goodman, Leo. A., and William H. Kruskal. "Measures of Association for Cross Classification." *Journal of the American Statistical Association,* 49 (December 1954), 732–764.

Hays, William L. *Statistics for Psychologists.* New York: Holt, 1963.

Jackson, Robert W. B. *Application of the Analysis of Variance and Covariance Method to Educational Problems.* Bulletin No. 11 of the Department of Educational Research, University of Toronto, 371 Bloor Street West, Toronto 5, Ontario, Canada, 1940.

Senders, Virginia L. *Measurement and Statistics.* New York: Oxford U. P., 1958.

Tables of the Binomial Probability Distribution. Washington, D.C.: Government Printing Office, 1949.

Tate, Merle W. *Statistics in Education and Psychology.* New York: Macmillan, 1965.

Terman, Lewis M., and Maud A. Merrill. *Stanford-Binet Intelligence Scale,* Manual for the Third Revision, Form L-M. Boston, Mass.: Houghton Mifflin, 1960.

Thorndike, Robert L., and Elizabeth P. Hagen. *Measurement*

and Evaluation in Psychology and Education. New York: Wiley, 1955. (Now in 3d ed.)

Wert, James E., Charles O. Neidt, and J. Stanley Ahmann. *Statistical Methods in Educational and Psychological Research.* New York: Appleton-Century-Crofts, 1954.

Index